KEYSTONE TOMBSTONES

Volume Three

Joe Farrell and Joe Farley

Mechanicsburg, Pennsylvania   USA

Published by Sunbury Press, Inc.
50 West Main Street, Suite A
Mechanicsburg, Pennsylvania 17055

www.sunburypress.com

Copyright © 2014 by Joe Farrell & Joe Farley.
Cover copyright © 2014 by Sunbury Press, Inc.

Sunbury Press supports copyright. Copyright fuels creativity, encourages diverse voices, promotes free speech, and creates a vibrant culture. Thank you for buying an authorized edition of this book and for complying with copyright laws by not reproducing, scanning, or distributing any part of it in any form without permission. You are supporting writers and allowing Sunbury Press to continue to publish books for every reader. For information contact Sunbury Press, Inc., Subsidiary Rights Dept., 50-A W. Main St., Mechanicsburg, PA 17011 USA or legal@sunburypress.com.

For information about special discounts for bulk purchases, please contact Sunbury Press Orders Dept. at (855) 338-8359 or orders@sunburypress.com.

To request one of our authors for speaking engagements or book signings, please contact Sunbury Press Publicity Dept. at publicity@sunburypress.com.

ISBN: 978-1-62006-361-3 (Trade Paperback)

FIRST SUNBURY PRESS EDITION: April 2014

Product of the United States of America
0 1 1 2 3 5 8 13 21 34 55

Set in Bookman Old Style
Designed by Lawrence Knorr
Cover by Lawrence Knorr
Edited by Allyson Gard
Cover image of Paterno statue by Bob and Holly Frymoyer

Continue the Enlightenment!

Acknowledgments

The success of *Keystone Tombstones Volumes One & Two* and the special edition of *Keystone Tombstones: Civil War* has led to this volume. We would like to thank all of those who purchased any of our books and encouraged us to continue this series.

Our work has been well-received and supported by many in the media, especially by Pennsylvania Cable Network (PCN). We'd like to thank Brian Lockman, Francine Schertzer, Corinna Wilson and Alanna Koll as well as the whole crew at PCN for their tremendous support and interest.

We are also grateful to Mike Rozansky and Tirdad Derakhshani of the *Philadelphia Inquirer* and Brian O'Neill of the *Pittsburgh Post-Gazette* for bringing our books to the attention of readers at both ends of the state.

We extend special thanks to Stacy Smith, Jill Neely, Kristine Sorenson and John Burnett for having us on "Pittsburgh Today Live" three times. We deeply appreciate it.

We also appreciate the interest, support and contributions of Paul Perrello of LaSalle TV in Philadelphia.

In Central Pennsylvania, we'd like to extend our thanks to Scott Lamar at WITF, and Chuck Rhodes and Amy Kehm at WHTM-TV, for their interest and support of our projects. We are also grateful to Debbie Beamer at the Mechanicsburg Mystery Bookshop and Dani Weller at the Harrisburg Midtown Scholar for their continued support.

Many others have been kind and supportive as we traveled around the state, often lost, often thirsty. Frank Rausch at Laurel Hill Cemetery and John Hopkins at Christ Church Preservation Trust, Jim Dino at the *Hazleton Standard-Speaker* and Terry Parris from PennLive were all particularly helpful.

We also want to thank Bob And Holly Frymoyer for providing us with the beautiful picture of the statue of Joe Paterno that is on the cover.

Lastly we thank our wives, Sharon Farley and Mary Farrell, for their tolerance of our folly. It's not easy being them.

Contents

Introduction 1
1. **Nick ADAMS** "Johnny Yuma Was a Rebel" 3
2. **Marian ANDERSON** "A Voice Heard Once in a Hundred Years" 7
3. **"Babes in the Woods"** 11
4. **John BARRYMORE** "The Great Profile" 17
5. **Robert CASEY** "The Three Time Loss from Holy Cross" 21
6. **Jimmy DORSEY** "A Fabulous Dorsey" 26
7. **FLIGHT 93 Crash Site** "40 Heroes" 30
8. **"Four Founders"** 36
9. **"Fox and Cox"** 45
10. **Joe William FRAZIER** "Smokin' Joe" 51
11. **Dave GARROWAY** "The Communicator" 57
12. **Harry GREB** "The Human Windmill" 61
13. **John Frederick HARTRANFT** "Old Johnny" 66
14. **Robert (Bob) HESS** "More than Just a Scientist" 71
15. **"The Kelayres Massacre"** 75
16. **John MCDERMOTT** "Golf's Unknown Champion" 79
17. **Mary Pinchot MEYER** "The Mysterious Case of Mary Pinchot Meyer" 85
18. **Joe PATERNO** "JoePa" 92
19. **Teddy PENDERGRASS** "Life Is a Song Worth Singing" 101
20. **Molly PITCHER** "From Molly Pitcher to Black Hawk Down" 106
21. **Art ROONEY** "The Chief" 112
22. **Lillian RUSSELL** "The Great American Beauty" 117
23. **Arlen SPECTER** "The Single Bullet Theory Senator" 122
24. **"Titanic Victims and Survivors"** 129
25. **Willie THROWER** "Football's Jackie Robinson" 145
26. **"Pirates' Pride"** 149
27. **John UPDIKE** "One of America's Best" 156
28. **Grover WASHINGTON, Jr.** "The Smooth Jazzman" 161
29. **Anthony WAYNE** "Mad Anthony" 164

Unusual Tombstones 172
Index 182

The information contained in this volume was obtained from multiple sources including internet sites, libraries, our personal book collections, magazines and newspapers.

Introduction

***The life of the dead is placed
in the memory of the living.***
Marcus Tullius Cicero

When Joe Farrell and I first got the idea to do a book called *Keystone Tombstones* back in the spring of 2010, we thought it would be just that one book. However, early on in that initial endeavor, we realized we had too much material for just one book. In addition, we began receiving suggestions from friends, family members and people we would meet on our travels of more people (that we didn't know about) that deserved inclusion in the book. In addition we added names to the list as people passed away, for example Joe Paterno, Arlen Specter, Smokin' Joe Frazier and Robert Hess are covered in this volume, but all four were still among the living when we published Volume 1. Thus we decided on multiple volumes. This is Volume 3 though it is the fourth book in the series with *Keystone Tombstones Civil War* being a special edition.

In keeping with the tone set in the previous volumes, there is a wide assortment of people covered in *Volume 3*. We have included great athletes, a legendary coach, politicians, entertainers, one of President Kennedy's lovers and more stories where tragedy is the theme including the Kelayres Massacre, Flight 93, Victims and Survivors of the Titanic that are buried in Pennsylvania and a story of three young girls who were found murdered in the woods near Carlisle. *Volume 3* does have a first in that this volume includes the story of a family member. Robert Hess was my father-in-law. When I told my wife Sharon that I was going to include him she said, "But he's not famous." In reply I used a point Joe Farrell makes when we do a presentation on the books, (yes, we are available). Farrell likes to point out that you don't have to be famous; you just had to have done something distinctive. I told my wife that the way her father lived his entire life was distinctive and that he remains one of the most impressive men I ever met. Thus he made the cut.

In keeping with our past practices we met and decided who we would cover in this volume. We then divided the potential chapters between us and went to work writing. Naturally we also made trips to the cemeteries to obtain photographs of the grave sites and other tributes made in memory of the people whose stories are told in the following pages. Once again the visits to the cemeteries, particularly those that don't have an office on the grounds, can be very challenging in locating the graves you are looking for.

Those of you who are familiar with our previous volumes will find the format much the same. We offer brief bios of the individuals or an explanation of the story involved with the grave site. We obtain this information from a number of sources including the internet, libraries and our own book collections. We have also included an "If You Go" section at the end of each chapter that tells of other graves in the cemetery you might want to visit. In addition, this section includes recommendations for eateries which are in the area that we visited on our trips and were happy with. Finally, as has been our practice, we visited as many Congressional Medal of Honor recipients as possible, and we have included photos of unusual graves we came upon.

Farrell and Farley

Once again we learned an awful lot in writing this volume. We believe there are great stories in the following pages. Some of the people covered you are already well acquainted with due to their fame. However there are many others whom you may be reading about for the first time. The fact that they are less famous today than in their heyday does not make their stories less interesting. In fact we believe it is quite the opposite.

So there you have it. We certainly hope you enjoy the stories and we encourage you if possible to visit some of the grave sites. For those of you who are wondering: yes, we still have plenty of people to cover in future volumes. As a matter of fact we have come up with an idea for book that may come as a surprise to those of you who have become fans of the series.

1.
Johnny Yuma Was a Rebel

Nick Adams
County: Columbia
Town: Berwick
Cemetery: Saints Cyril and Methodius Ukrainian Cemetery
Address: Crystal Hill Road

He was an actor who appeared in a number of significant films including "Mister Roberts," "Giant" and "Rebel Without a Cause." He was nominated for an Academy Award for Best Supporting Actor in the 1963 film "Twilight of Honor," but the award went to Melvyn Douglas. He is best known for playing the role of Johnny Yuma in the television series "The Rebel." His name was Nick Adams.

Adams was born Nicholas Aloysius Adamshock on July 10, 1931, in Nanticoke, Pennsylvania. His father, Peter Adamshock, was a Ukrainian born coal miner. When Adams was five years old, his uncle was killed in a mining accident, and as a result, Adams's father moved the family to Jersey City, New Jersey.

Peter Adamshock got a job as a janitor in an apartment building. One of the jobs perks was that it came with living quarters in the basement. During this period Adams's mother went to work for Western Electric.

When young Nick was still in high school, he received an offer from the Saint Louis Cardinals to play minor league baseball. He turned that offer down because he didn't feel the job paid enough. It's been said that as a teenager he made money by hustling pool games. Money was obviously important to him. When his father urged him to pursue a trade, he responded by saying he wanted to do something where he could make a lot of money and that he couldn't do that with a trade. So it could be said that the pursuit of wealth is what led to his decision to get into acting.

In 1947 Adams, who was 17 at the time, visited New York City. He went into a theater where an audition was being held for a play called "The Silver Tassie." It was here that he met the actor Jack Palance who, like Adams, hailed from the coal country of northeastern Pennsylvania and was of Ukrainian descent. When Palance asked Adams why he wanted to be an actor the answer he got was for the money. Palance, who had changed his name from Jack Palahniuk, introduced Adams to the director as Nick Adams. Adams failed to land a part in the play, but Palance directed him to a junior theater group where he got an acting job playing the role of Muff Potter in "Tom Sawyer." During this time, Adams auditioned for a role in the play Mister Roberts where he met the legendary actor Henry Fonda. Fonda advised Adams to take some acting lessons. After a year in New York City, Adams hitchhiked across the country to Los Angeles.

Once he reached Los Angeles, Adams worked as a doorman, usher and maintenance man at the Warners Theater in Beverly Hills. His first paid acting job was in a stage play called "Mr. Big Shot." His first film role came in 1951 in a movie titled

Photo of Nick Adams in a guest-starring role on the television program The Monroes.

"Somebody Loves Me." The following year he was drafted into the United States Coast Guard.

In June of 1954 Adams auditioned in his Coast Guard uniform for the famed director John Ford. The effort earned him the part of Seaman Reber in the film "Mister Roberts." Adams completed his military service and upon his return to Los Angeles, based on his work in "Mister Roberts," he signed a contract with the Warner Brothers studio.

In 1955 Adams landed a role in the movie "Rebel Without a Cause" He befriended the stars of the movie James Dean and Natalie Wood. During breaks in the filming Dean and Adams would entertain the cast by imitating movie stars such as Marlon Brando. When Dean was killed in an automobile accident in 1955, Adams overdubbed some of Dean's lines for the film "Giant." Adams attempted to cash in on Dean's death by writing articles about Dean for movie magazines. In addition he claimed that he had adopted Dean's habits when it came to fast cars, claiming he had been arrested for speeding nine times in one year.

In the late 1950s, Adams' career began to blossom. He appeared in a number of successful television shows such as "Wanted: Dead or Alive" which starred Steve McQueen. In addition he appeared in films including "No Time for Sergeants" and "Pillow Talk."

In 1959 Adams was cast to star in a television series titled "The Rebel." Adams's character was named Johnny Yuma, an ex-Confederate soldier who wandered through the west toting a sawed off shotgun. Adams had hoped to get his friend Elvis Presley to sing the title song for the show, but the producer picked Johnny Cash. The show was a hit and 76 half-hour episodes were filmed before it was canceled at the end of the 1961 season.

In 1964 Adams appeared in an episode of the television show "The Outer Limits." Critics would later point to this performance as proof that he was underrated as an actor. In 1964 he co-starred in the movie "Young Dillinger" but the critics panned the movie and it flopped.

It was around this time that Adams' career began to go downhill. In 1965, after publicly declaring that he would not work on films that were produced outside the United States, he accepted parts in Japanese science fiction films including "Frankenstein Conquers the World" and the 6th Godzilla film "Invasion of Astro-Monster." During this period he also starred in a film with Boris Karloff that was filmed in England called "Die, Monster, Die!" In 1967 Adams would appear in a Disney release titled "Mosby's Marauders." He also appeared in a number of television series including "The Wild Wild West" and "Combat." In 1968 he was cast to star in a low budget science fiction film called "Mission Mars" which critics described as being "utterly dreadful." His last production in the United States was a stock car movie titled "Fever Heat." His last appearance on film was in a Spanish language western called "Los Asesinos."

Adams married a former child actress named Carol Nugent in 1959. The couple had two children, Allyson Lee Adams and Jeb Stuart Adams. The relationship between Adams and his wife was a rocky one. By 1965, they were separated, and the children were living with Carol. In November of 1966 Carol initiated divorce proceedings and obtained a restraining order against Adams.

On the night of February 7, 1968 Adams failed to show up for a dinner appointment he had made with his lawyer Erwin Roeder. Roeder drove to Adams

Unique grave of the underrated movie and TV star Nick Adams.

The authors with Norbert O'Donnell, the owner of the O'Donnell winery in Berwick.

Beverly Hills home to check on the actor. He broke a window to gain entry and found Adams in his upstairs bedroom in a sitting position leaning against a wall dead. Adams was 36 years old.

The coroner Dr. Thomas Noguchi determined that the cause of death was "paraldehyde and promazine intoxication." He was unable to determine if the death was accidental or a suicide. Over the years Adams' children have speculated that foul play may have been involved in the death of their father. Adams' best friend, actor Robert Conrad, has always felt that the death was accidental. Adams was laid to rest in the Saints Cyril and Methodius Ukrainian Cemetery in Berwick, Pennsylvania.

Adams' death at such a young age has made him part of what's been called the curse of "Rebel Without a Cause." The curse is based on the fact that four of the cast members of that film passed away at a very young age. As mentioned previously, in addition to Adams, James Dean died in an automobile accident at the age of 24. Another star in the movie was Sal Mineo who was stabbed to death on February 12, 1976 while he was walking home from a rehearsal for a play. He was 37 years old. Finally the female lead in the movie, Natalie Wood, drowned on February 28, 1981. Wood was 43 years old at the time of her death.

If You Go:

The authors suggest a visit to "The O'Donnell Winery" located at 25 Hayes Road in Berwick. The wines are tasty, and the owners are very friendly and eager to do all they can to meet your needs. In addition, weather permitting there is outside seating in a beautiful setting where you can watch the Susquehanna River flow by as you enjoy the fine wines.

2.
A Voice Heard Once in a Hundred Years

Marian Anderson
Town: Collingdale
Cemetry: Eden Cemetary
Address: 1434 Springfield Road

She performed throughout Europe and the United States. She was a prominent figure in the struggle to overcome racial prejudice during her life time. She gave a legendary concert on Easter Sunday in 1939 on the steps of the Lincoln Memorial. For years she worked as a delegate to the United Nations Human Rights Committee. She performed at President John F. Kennedy's inauguration in 1961. She returned to the Lincoln Memorial to sing during the March on Washington in 1963. After one her performances Arturo Toscanini told her "Yours is a voice one hears once in a hundred years." Her name was Marian Anderson.

Anderson was born on February 27, 1897 in Philadelphia. Her father, John Anderson whose own father had been a slave, sold ice and coal before opening a liquor store. Her mother Annie earned money by taking care of neighborhood children. Anderson had two younger sisters Alice and Ethel. Ethel's son James Anderson DePriest became an accomplished conductor.

Anderson's family was active in the Union Baptist Church in Philadelphia. One of Anderson's aunts convinced the six year old girl to join the junior church choir. Anderson later gave her aunt credit for influencing her to pursue a career in music. When she was in her early teens, she was paid up to $5.00 to sing a few songs at various functions. She also gained the notice of the tenor Roland Hayes who provided her with guidance with her developing career.

Anderson first experienced racism when she tried to be admitted to a local music school. The young girl who handled her application shocked Anderson with the words that came out of her mouth. Anderson described the experience as being like having, a cold, horrifying hand laid on her. She said she didn't argue with the girl; instead she turned and walked out.

Anderson then pursued her music studies by receiving private lessons from Giuseppe Boghetti and Agnes Reifsynder. Her pastor along with other leaders of the black community raised money to pay for the lessons.

In 1925 Anderson won a singing competition sponsored by the New York Philharmonic. As a result, she earned the right to perform with the Philharmonic, and her appearance met with critical acclaim. Around this time, Arthur Judson, whom she met through the Philharmonic, became her manager. In the following years, she made numerous appearances in the United States, but she felt that racial prejudice was preventing her career from really moving forward. She decided to go to Europe where she launched a highly successful concert tour.

Marian Anderson in 1940, by Carl Van Vechten

It was in 1930 that she performed for the first time in Europe. The concert took place in London, and it was a tremendous success. Because she didn't encounter the prejudice that she had in America, she spent most of the early 1930's touring Europe. In 1930 Anderson met the pianist Kosti Vehanen, and he became both her vocal coach and accompanist for a number of years. Through Vehanen, she met Jean Sibelius who heard her perform in Helsinki. The two formed a friendship, and for years Sibelius composed music for Anderson to perform.

In 1934 Anderson hired Sol Hurok to manage her career because he made her an offer that was better than the one she had with Arthur Jackson. Hurok would remain her manager for the rest of her career, and he was instrumental in convincing her to return to the United States to perform. In 1935 she performed in New York at Town Hall. Once again, her concert earned numerous positive reviews. Anderson successfully toured the United States for the next four years. By the late 1930's Anderson was performing around seventy concerts a year in the states. By this time she was very famous, but that fame did not translate into acceptance everywhere in America. She was still denied service by many hotels and restaurants throughout the country. As a matter of fact, there were many times Albert Einstein acted as her host, the first time being in 1937 when she couldn't get a hotel room before a performance at Princeton University. He last hosted her in 1955 shortly before he passed away.

It was in 1939 that the Daughters of the American Revolution (DAR) refused to allow Anderson to perform before an integrated audience in their Constitution Hall. As a result of that decision many DAR members, including First Lady Eleanor Roosevelt, resigned from the organization. President Roosevelt and others arranged for Anderson to perform in an open air concert on the steps of the Lincoln Memorial. The concert attracted a crowd of over 75,000 people, and millions of others heard it over the radio.

When World War II broke out, Anderson made it a point to entertain the troops. She did the same thing during the Korean War. In 1943 the DAR invited her to perform at Constitution Hall. She accepted the invitation and said it was no different than singing at other venues. She didn't gloat over her victory; she simply said she was happy to sing there.

On July 17, 1943, Anderson became the second wife of a man who had proposed to her when they were teenagers. His name was Orpheus Fisher, and he was an architect. After they were married, the couple purchased a 100 acre farm in Danbury, Connecticut. They had also searched for homes in New York and New Jersey and had attempted to make some purchases, but the sellers would remove their homes from the market when they found out it was a black couple that were the buyers.

In 1955 Anderson became the first African-American performer to appear with the Metropolitan Opera in New York. Afterward she was made a permanent member of the company. The following year she authored her autobiography titled *My Lord, What a Morning*. The book became a bestseller.

In 1957, she sang at the inauguration of President Dwight Eisenhower. Four years later she sang at the inauguration of President Kennedy. In 1962 she again sang for Kennedy this time at the White House. She was also very active in the civil rights movement during this period. She gave concerts to benefit the Congress of Racial Equality and the National Association for the Advancement of Colored People. In 1963 she became one of the original recipients of the Presidential Medal of Freedom. In 1965 she was chosen to christen the nuclear submarine the USS George Washington Carver.

Modest grave of a woman who had a voice was heard once in a hundred years.

That same year she concluded her farewell tour, and her final concert took place at Carnegie Hall in April.

Back on the farm in Connecticut, she refused to be treated as a celebrity. She refused offers to move to the front of waiting lines at local restaurants. When her local town lit the Christmas lights, she sang at city hall. She also performed at the local high school.

After she retired, honors continued to come her way. She received the University of Pennsylvania Glee Club Award of Merit in 1973. In 1977 she was presented with the United Nations Peace Prize. The following year she received the Kennedy Center Honors and in 1986 the National Medal of Arts award. In 1991 the Grammy's presented her with a Lifetime Achievement Award. In addition she was awarded honorary doctoral degrees from Howard University, Temple University and Smith College.

After 43 years of marriage Anderson's husband passed away in 1986. She remained in the residence until 1992 which was one year before her death. Anderson died of congestive heart failure on April 8, 1993; she was 96 years old. In 2002 the author Molefi Kete Asante listed Anderson in his book *100 Greatest African Americans*.

If You Go:

Should you decide to visit Marian Anderson you are close to Philadelphia which is an historical Mecca. We have visited many graves in this area that are included in Volumes One and Two and in our special Civil War Edition. You should also check out the If You Go section in this volume in the chapter titled *Four Founders*. It goes without saying that Philadelphia offers numerous attractions and great places to eat and drink.

3.
Babes in the Woods

Norma Sedgwick
Dewilla Noakes
Cordelia Noakes

Elmo Noakes
Winifred Pierce

County: Cumberland
Town: Carlisle
Cemetery: Westminster Memorial Gardens
Address: 1159 Newville Road

Sadly, the authors are old enough to have been raised by parents who lived during the Great Depression. I remember hearing lots of stories from my parents and grandparents about how tough times were and how much people suffered during "The Depression." I think I was in high school before I learned that "depression" could be an economic term. Until then, I thought it was called "The Depression" because so many people were depressed emotionally as a result of the hard times. The story of the Babes in the Woods is perhaps illustrative of just how bad things were during that time.

On November 24, 1934, two men were in the woods near Carlisle intending to cut some firewood when they saw a mound covered with a green blanket. Clark Jardine and John Clark thought it was an odd thing to see in the woods and by the looks of it, it hadn't been there very long. They decided to check it out and were horrified at what they found. Under the blanket were the bodies of three young girls. The two men went in search of a telephone and called the police in Carlisle. The police arrived shortly and so did a crowd, some seeking children of their own who had gone missing.

The girls looked like they were almost certainly related to one another. The Carlisle chief of police speculated that they were probably sisters. They were dressed in nice outfits, including coats. No one knew or had any idea who the girls were. A Dickinson College professor analyzed pieces of their hair and corroborated the speculation that they were sisters. The bodies had no wounds or marks on them other than a small mark on the forehead of one girl. This mark launched police on a search for a possible secret society whose symbol might have been marked on the child. This led nowhere. The sad mystery of the three girls swept the nation.

The quest for the girls' identity started a nationwide media frenzy. The photographs of the children lying on a blanket at the site were printed in newspapers across the country. Thousands came to view the bodies in hopes of identifying them. Death masks were made before burial to continue the search. The media frenzy led to many false leads for the police.

Five days after the bodies were discovered, a black leather suitcase was found in brush about three miles from the point where the bodies had been located. A man named John Naugle, of New Cumberland, had found the suitcase. It contained clothing

The bodies of Norma, Dewilla and Cordelia Noakes, collectively known as the "Babes in the Woods," were found Nov. 24, 1934. (Pennsylvania State Police)

similar to that worn by the three small girls, as well as a notebook with the name "Norma" written on it, in what appeared to be a youngster's handwriting.

Shortly after the girls' bodies surfaced, the bodies of a man and woman were found in an abandoned railroad flag stop about 100 miles away in Duncansville, PA, just south of Altoona. The woman had been shot in the heart and the head, and the man had been shot in the head. A few days later a 1929 blue Pontiac sedan was found abandoned in a field near McVeytown, in Mifflin County. The car had no license plates and was out of gas. Its engine number had been intentionally obscured.

The car was traced to a man by the name of Elmo Noakes. The description of the car, the physical features of the bodies and Elmo Noakes' fingerprints from U.S. Marine records led to identification of the bodies as being that of Noakes (31 years old at the time of his death) and Winifred Pierce (age 18), formerly of Roseville, California. Pierce was also identified from pictures and by the fact that she had a deformed left foot.

Elmo Noakes was born on January 8, 1903 in Springville, Utah. He and his brother Robert served in the Marines from 1920 to 1922. In July 1923, he married a woman named Mary Hayford. Mary had a daughter named Norma Sedgwick from a previous marriage. Mary and Elmo had two children together: daughters Dewilla (born May 2, 1924) and Cordelia (born June 2, 1926).

In 1932, Mary died from infection following a self-induced abortion in Salt Lake City, Utah. Subsequently, Elmo moved to Roseville, California, where his three sisters could help care for and raise Norma, Dewilla and Cordelia. He was employed by Pacific Fruit Express, a railroad fruit shipping company.

Winifred "Winnie" Pierce was born on September 1, 1916 in Utah, to father Hugh Pierce and mother Pearl Noakes (Elmo's oldest sister, thus making Elmo Winifred's uncle, and she his niece). Winifred moved to Roseville and attended high school there. After high school, she went to work as a housekeeper for Elmo. How she and Elmo and his three daughters wound up lying dead on Pennsylvania soil would prove to be an interesting challenge for investigators in the Keystone State, who were essentially left with no choice other than to start working backwards in the hopes of piecing together what may have transpired.

The girls' bodies were taken to the Ewing Funeral Home on South Hanover Street in Carlisle. An autopsy revealed that the children had had nothing to eat for at least 18 hours prior to their deaths. A pathologist at Harrisburg Hospital, George Moffitt, tested sections of the girls' organs and determined that they had not died of carbon monoxide poisoning, and that they had not been sexually assaulted. Another postmortem exam failed to find any indications of poison in the girls' systems.

Brothers Robert and Elmo Noakes served in the U.S. Marine Corps during World War I.

If the girls could not be identified, they would be buried in a potter's field. State police asked the PA Board of Education to inquire about missing children of every school in Pennsylvania. Finally, three people came forward who claimed to have seen a man and a woman together with the three children in a restaurant in Philadelphia on November 19. The restaurant was the LaSalle Sandwich Shoppe on North Broad Street. The owner, Louis Ellis, remembered talking to Elmo Noakes about looking for work and Noakes saying he would take anything he could get. He mentioned his family was getting to be a "pretty big burden."

A waitress at the restaurant, Ann Gasparon, seated the party of five at two tables, and remembered that they ordered only one meal to be shared by all of them. A customer sitting nearby with her eight-year-old son heard this and felt sorry for the children. Anna LaFauvre invited the girls to join her and her son for a meal. The youngest Noakes child did, and they had a nice conversation. The girl told Mrs. LaFauvre they were from California and that she was in the third grade.

After the discovery of the bodies, all three adult witnesses from the restaurant were brought to Carlisle to assist in identifying the deceased children. Mrs. LaFauvre identified the bodies and fainted. Ellis and Gasparon also identified the girls as the ones they had seen in the restaurant. They were all driven to view the adult decedents and again recognized the bodies. As a result, the papers printed their identities on November 30, 1934 as:

Cordelia Noakes, age 8
Dewilla Noakes, age 10
Norma Sedgwick, age 13
Elmo Noakes, age 32
Winifred Pierce, age 18

On December 1, the funeral for the girls was held at Ewing Funeral Home. Hundreds of people attended, despite a heavy rain. The funeral/burial was paid for by the American Legion Post, apparently because Elmo Noakes had been a Marine. Boy scouts and girl scouts served as pallbearers. Presbyterian, Catholic and Episcopal clergy all participated. The burial was in Westminster Cemetery. A stone monument marks their burial spot.

Days later, Elmo Noakes and Winifred Pierce were also buried in Westminster Cemetery, about 100 yards from the girls in separate graves. The American Legion provided for Elmo's funeral and a bugler played "Taps" over his grave. At that time, his role in the girls' deaths had not been established. Winnie's funeral was paid for by a sister.

Norma Sedgwick's father, Rowland, had tried to gain custody of his daughter after Mary Noakes died. He failed in his efforts and now he could not even afford to have her body transported to Utah where he lived. He was reportedly heartbroken.

In 1968, a group of Pennsylvania highway workers on their own time and initiative erected a blue and yellow keystone-shaped sign along Route 233 where the childrens' bodies were found. It reads:

ON THIS SPOT
WERE FOUND THREE
BABES IN THE WOODS
NOV. - 24 - 1934

This sign on a rural Pennsylvania road marks the spot where the bodies of the three young girls were found.

We will never know for sure what happened. A State Police investigation concluded that Elmo Noakes left Roseville, California on November 11, 1934, with the three children and Winifred Pierce. Eleven days prior to their departure, on October 31, Noakes had purchased a blue 1929 Pontiac sedan for $46. Police theorized that he ran out of money and without prospects of employment killed the girls on November 21 rather than let them starve. It is generally believed that Noakes killed his daughters by suffocating them while they slept.

Then (the theory goes), after leaving the girls' bodies on blankets in the woods, Noakes and Pierce drove west, abandoned their car when it ran out of gas between McVeytown and Altoona, and hitchhiked to Altoona. On November 23, Pierce sold her coat, which was the couple's last possession except for the clothes they were wearing. Noakes bought a .22-caliber rifle from a second-hand store with the $2.55 Pierce got for her coat, and on November 24 used it to kill Pierce and then himself. The weapon was found lying between their bodies. They spent their last night together at the Congress Hotel at 118th Street in Altoona, where the woman who ran the hotel confirmed afterwards that she had indeed rented them a room for all the money they had on them: 48 cents.

By all accounts, Elmo Noakes had a good reputation, a job, loved and cared for the girls, and had a non-violent nature. There are many strange elements to this story - elements on which one can only speculate. For instance, the group left California three days *before* Noakes would have gotten a paycheck for two weeks' work - money that would have come in extremely handy for a group of people about to embark on a cross-country trip. The speculation is that family strife caused them to leave suddenly. News accounts report that Noakes' sisters cared for his daughters at first, that is up until the time Elmo hired his niece, Winnie, to be his housekeeper and take care of the girls. Winnie started by working at Elmo's house in the day and returning to her home at her mother's house in the evening. After about six months however, Winnie quit going home and moved in with Elmo.

The gossip in the community was that the relationship between uncle and niece had turned romantic, and two of Noakes' sisters strongly objected, even threatening to get the children removed from the household. Soon none of Elmo's sisters would speak to him. There was also acrimony between Winnie's mother, Pearl, and her husband, Hugh, over the situation. After the bodies were found, two of Noakes' sisters were found guilty of disturbing the peace stemming from their harassment of Pearl who they blamed for the deaths. Perhaps the turmoil reached a breaking point and led to impulsive, reckless behavior.

This tombstone marks the spot where the babes were laid to rest.

Here is the grave of Elmo Knoakes who took his own life after killing his three daughters.

Also puzzling is the fact that - despite Elmo claiming to be looking for work - they traveled very fast across the country, and there were no reports of Noakes or Pierce actually asking for work. Their feeble attempts to avoid identification are also odd. The effacing of the car's VIN number, the discarding of the license plates, the use of aliases at places they stayed, the couples' manner of travel after leaving the bodies - these things all beg for explanations that won't ever be known for certain. Yet even after nearly 80 years, the memory of those beautiful young girls remains as haunting as ever.

If You Go:

Westminster Memorial Gardens is the final resting place for two American heroes:

John W. Minick, who was a staff sergeant in the United States Army when he was killed in action near Hurtgen, Germany, on November 21, 1944. On that day, he voluntarily led a small group of men through a minefield, single-handedly silenced two enemy machine gun emplacements, and engaged a company of German soldiers before he was killed while crossing a second minefield. For his actions he was awarded the Medal of Honor. His citation reads that he killed 22 enemy soldiers and captured 23 more. He was 36 years old.

Randall D. Shughart, who was a Special Forces soldier from Newville, Pennsylvania, and one of two soldiers (the other being Gary Gordon) who died trying to save the life of pilot Michael Durant, the only surviving member of a downed helicopter crew in Somalia on October 3, 1993. Shughart's actions - while costing him his own life - saved Durant's. For those actions, Shughart was awarded the Medal of Honor by President Clinton - the first soldier to be posthumously awarded the Medal of Honor since the Vietnam War. This incident was featured in the book and blockbuster Hollywood film "Black Hawk Down." The movie won two Oscars and was nominated for two more.

Shughart has been memorialized in many ways. A United States Navy ship, a training facility in Fort Polk, Louisiana, and his hometown post office in Newville all bear his name. Twenty years after his death, his modest grave was enhanced with a monument in his memory.

Also in Carlisle is the **Old Public Graveyard** (South Bedford & East South Streets), where **Molly Pitcher** and a number of **Revolutionary War figures** are buried (see Chapter 20).

A very short distance from Westminster Memorial Gardens is the **Rustic Tavern** (823 Newville Road). We stopped in for lunch and were hoping the experience would pick up our spirits. It was a cold, gloomy day and the story of the "Babes in the Woods" had proven to be equally cold and gloomy. It worked! The food, service and ambiance were all great. We warmed ourselves by the fire, had a hearty lunch and some spirits, and left determined to live on.

4.
The Great Profile

John Barrymore
County: Philadelphia
Town: Philadelphia
Cemetery: Mount Vernon Cemetery
Address: Intersection of Ridge and Lehigh Avenue

He was born into an acting family. He first made a name for himself on stage starting with light comedy and then appearing in dramas. He was especially praised for his work in Shakespearean plays. From the stage he moved to the silver screen where he met with immediate and great success. He was envied for his good looks which earned him the moniker "the Great Profile." His name was John Barrymore.

Barrymore was born on February 15, 1882, in Philadelphia. His father, Herbert Arthur Chamberlayne Blythe, was a British actor who performed under the name Maurice Barrymore. His mother, Georgie Drew Barrymore, was an actress as well. Barrymore had a brother Lionel and a sister Ethel. His maternal grandmother was Louisa Lane Drew who was also an actress and theatre manager. Drew was instrumental in directing all three siblings into acting. Growing up in such a theatrical family resulted in Barrymore meeting some of the leading actors of the day including Edwin Booth.

While he was still in his teens he dated the showgirl Evelyn Nesbitt (See chapter on Harry Thaw in *Keystone Tombstones Volume 2*). There were rumors that Nesbitt had become pregnant and that Barrymore arranged for her to have an abortion. In 1906, Nesbitt's husband Harry Thaw shot one of her former lovers, the noted architect Stanford White, to death on the rooftop of Madison Square Garden. Questions were prepared to ask Barrymore at the trial the purpose of which was to attack Nesbitt's character. The trial however was settled by an insanity plea and Barrymore was never called to the stand.

Initially Barrymore attempted to avoid following in his parents footsteps by trying to make a living as a reporter and a cartoonist. He went to art school and worked for several New York newspapers before he made the decision to become an actor. He made his stage debut in 1903 at the Cleveland Theatre in Chicago. He then moved on to Broadway where he performed for two years before heading to England to appear in a play called "The Dictator."

In 1906 Barrymore was staying in a hotel in San Francisco when the earthquake hit. He was starring in a production of "The Dictator" and was set to go to Australia to tour in that play. Barrymore had no desire to make that trip so he went into hiding spending the next few days at the house of a friend where he went on a drinking binge. While he was drinking he came up with an idea as to how he could use the earthquake for his own benefit. He posed as a reporter and simply made up scenes he claimed to

John Barrymore

have witnessed. Years later in a letter to his sister he admitted he had done so. When the information became public it did Barrymore no harm as by that time he was widely known and admired for his talent.

In 1910, Barrymore married an actress named Katherine Corri Harris. It was the first of his four marriages, and the couple divorced in 1917. By 1912, Barrymore was the American actor who ruled the American stage. It was at this highpoint in his career that he decided to make motion pictures. He began to make films at that time but he still worked on Broadway. In 1913 he made the decision to abandon the stage in order to make films full time. That same year he starred in the silent film "An American Citizen."

At first Barrymore concentrated on making light comedies. A friend of his convinced him to try his hand at drama. In 1916 he appeared in a film called "Justice" to critical acclaim. One of his co-stars was Cathleen Nesbitt who would introduce him to his second wife Blanche Oelrichs. They would marry in 1920 and divorce in 1925. The union would produce one child a daughter named Diana Blanche Barrymore. Diana would die at that age of 38 from an overdose of alcohol combined with sleeping pills. Barrymore would make a movie with Errol Flynn called "Too Much, Too Soon" based on her life.

When World War 1 saw the United States enter the fray in 1917, Barrymore, who was 35 at the time, tried to enlist in the armed forces. He failed the physical due to varicose veins. That same year he returned to Broadway to star in a play called "Peter Ibbetson" in a role his father had always wanted to play. In 1919 he starred with his brother Lionel in "The Jest." Then it was back to Shakespeare when he appeared in "Richard III" in 1920. This was followed by what many consider his greatest stage triumph, his starring role in "Hamlet" in 1922. The play ran for 101 performances, and Barrymore broke the record for consecutive appearances that had been held by Edwin Booth.

Barrymore closed out his silent film career by appearing in a number of successful films. These included "Dr. Jekyll and Mr. Hyde" (the band Queen used scenes from this film in their music video Under Pressure), "Sherlock Holmes" and "Don Juan."

In 1928 he married the model and actress Dolores Costello. They were divorced in 1935. The union produced two children a girl born in 1930 named Dolores Ethel Mae Barrymore and a son born in 1932 named John Drew Barrymore. John is the father of the actress Drew Barrymore.

Talking pictures proved to be a big plus for Barrymore. His debut in talkies was a dramatic reading of the Duke of Gloucester's speech from "Henry VI." Clearly Barrymore's stage trained voice fit perfectly with talking pictures. In 1930 he reprised a role he had played in a silent film starring as Captain Ahab in "Moby Dick." He then made a few movies with his brother Lionel including "Arsene Lupin," "The Mad Genius" and in 1932 "Grand Hotel." In addition to the Barrymore's the latter film featured an all-star cast that included Joan Crawford and Greta Garbo. That same year the brothers starred in "Rasputin and the Princess" followed by "Dinner at Eight" in 1933.

Over the years Barrymore appeared with most of the leading ladies of the time including Myrna Loy, Katherine Hepburn and Jean Harlow. In the 1933 film "Counsellor at Law" Barrymore portrayed a Jewish attorney. The film critic Pauline Kael would later praise this performance calling it "one of the few screen roles that reveal his measure as an actor." She added that his "presence is apparent in every scene; so are his restraint, his humor and his zest."

In the 30's Barrymore's return to the stage met with much success. He actually inspired several plays including "The Royal family" and "My Dear Children." Both of these plays would become films. He also served as the inspiration for two films "Sing Baby Sing" and "The Great Profile." In 1936 he gave a critically praised performance playing Mercutio in "Romeo and Juliet." That same year he was married for the fourth and final time to Elaine Barrie an actress, the two would divorce in 1940.

In 1937 he appeared in a film with Jeanette MacDonald called "Maytime." It became the top grossing film of the year worldwide. It is still regarded as one of the best film musicals of the 1930's.

In the late 30's Barrymore began losing the ability to remember his lines. As a result when he made films they were forced to use cue cards. His films began losing money and by 1938 he was considered box office poison along with others such as Fred Astaire and Joan Crawford.

Barrymore collapsed while appearing on Rudy Vallee's Radio show in 1942. He was rushed to the hospital. He had been a smoker his whole life and also suffered from chronic alcoholism, heart problems and pneumonia. According to one of his biographers Barrymore roused and tried to say something to his brother Lionel, and Lionel asked him to repeat what he had said and Barrymore replied, "You heard me, Mike." He then met death with a smile on May 29, 1942. According to Errol Flynn's memoirs the film director Roaul Walsh took Barrymore's body and placed it in a chair in Flynn's house, left to be discovered by Flynn when he returned home from a night of drinking. Walsh said the story was true in a 1973 documentary called "The Men Who Made the Movies." The story was challenged by a friend of Barrymore's who claimed that he and his son stayed with the body at the funeral right up to the burial. Among Barrymore's pallbearers were W. C. Fields, Louis B. Mayer and David O. Selznick. He was laid to rest in Mount Vernon Cemetery in Philadelphia.

For his work in films Barrymore was awarded a star on the Hollywood Walk of Fame. Unlike his sister Ethel and his brother Lionel he never won an Academy Award. However all three siblings have been inducted into the American Theatre Hall of Fame.

Barrymore was a good friend and drinking Buddy of W. C. Fields. In the 1976 film, "W. C. Fields and Me," Barrymore was portrayed by Jack Cassidy. He is also mentioned in the song "I May Be Wrong (But I think You're Wonderful)" which was recorded by a number of artists including Doris Day.

If You Go:

What can we say except that attempting to visit this grave site proved to be a first for us. I suppose we can begin by telling you that you need to call the cemetery at least 24 hours before you visit to make an appointment. This is necessary because the grounds are locked and someone needs to meet you there in order for you to gain entrance. When we called we spoke to a man who identified himself as the owner of the property. We informed him of who we wanted to visit and he asked us if we were relatives. We told him no and explained the reason for our visit. He responded by telling us that we would need to pay a fee to photograph the grave. He said that according to his attorney the site was his "intellectual property." We chose not to pay so this marks the first grave included in this series that we were unable to visit. We hope our readers have better luck and we continue to wonder what Drew Barrymore might think of the stand taken by the owner with regard to our attempt to visit her grandfather's grave.

5.
The Three Time Loss from Holy Cross

Robert Casey
County: Lackawanna
Town: Moscow
Cemetery: Saint Catherine's
Address: Route 435 and Main Street

He had run unsuccessfully for the office of Governor of Pennsylvania three times before he won the 1986 election. He practically went to war with his own party over the issue of abortion, a procedure he staunchly opposed. In 1993 he underwent a controversial and rare heart-liver transplant. His name was Robert P. Casey.

Casey was born on January 9, 1932, in New York City. His family was originally from Scranton Pennsylvania, and they would eventually return there. Casey attended Scranton Preparatory School where he excelled as an athlete on both the baseball and basketball teams. As a matter of fact after he graduated, the Philadelphia Phillies wanted to sign him to a contract, but he decided to accept a basketball scholarship and attend college at Holy Cross. After graduation Casey went to George Washington University where he earned a law degree.

In 1962 Casey was elected to the Pennsylvania State Senate as a democrat from Lackawanna County. In 1964 he was present at the party's Saint Patrick's Day dinner where Robert Kennedy made his first public appearance since the assassination of his brother. In 1966 he made his first run for governor. Although he was the choice of the party professionals he was defeated in the primary election by Milton Shapp. He would repeat the loss to Shapp in 1970 and in 1978 he was defeated in the primary by Pete Flaherty. He was successful in both 1968 and 1972 when he was elected to the position of Pennsylvania's Auditor General.

Even though he was unsuccessful in his runs for governor, the name Bob Casey was popular among Pennsylvania voters. In 1976 a man who was also named Bob Casey ran for the office of State Treasurer. Although he spent little money and hardly campaigned at all he won the election. In 1978 yet another Bob Casey won the Democratic party's nomination for the office of Lieutenant Governor.

The real Bob Casey had left his post as Auditor General because of term limits. He spent the next decade practicing law. In 1986 he decided to run for Governor of Pennsylvania for the fourth time. Many called him the three time loss from Holy Cross. Casey hired two virtually unknown political strategists to plan his campaign. Their names were James Carville and Paul Begala. Billing himself as the real Bob Casey, he won the Democratic primary. In the general election, he faced Pennsylvania's Lieutenant Governor, a son of a previous Pennsylvania Governor by the name of Bill Scranton. Needless to say whoever won the election would hail from Scranton, Pennsylvania. Most pundits would predict the Scranton would emerge the winner in the general election.

Robert Patrick Casey, Sr. (January 9, 1932 – May 30, 2000) (Photo taken by Michael Casey)

John Baer, in his excellent book *On the Front Lines of Pennsylvania Politics*, explains what he felt made the difference in the election. Baer agreed to work for Scranton as his press secretary. It is his view that the election was decided by three events. According to Baer, the first occurred in the state capital newsroom where Scranton appeared before reporters to deliver uplifting economic news showing that Pennsylvania was moving in the right direction. Toward the end of the press conference Scranton was asked about his endorsement of Bob Casey for Auditor General in 1972. At the time Scranton was running three weekly newspapers in the Pennsylvania northeastern coal region. Scranton responded by basically saying that one of the nice things about getting older was moving past your youthful indiscretions. Another reporter asked a follow up question saying speaking of youthful indiscretions any comment on drug use. Scranton left without answering the question. Within a few hours the press was all over the story. Eventually he admitted that in his youth he used recreational drugs.

According to Baer, the second pitfall took place when Scranton decided to take the high road and cease any negative political advertising. Initially the strategy appeared to work as the Scranton campaign received media praise. Then it all fell apart when the campaign sent out a direct mailer to 600,000 Pennsylvanians charging that Casey ignored fraud and corruption in state government while he was auditor general. The ad also claimed that during this period Casey was making $100,000 practicing law rather than attending to his public duties. The latter part of the ad was false as Casey made the money over a four year period. The story was picked up by Pennsylvania newspapers, and the Casey campaign labeled Scranton a hypocrite.

Scranton took the Casey campaign's final punch on the Friday before Election Day. Casey and Carville began airing what would become known as the "guru ad." The ad attacked Scranton for practicing transcendental meditation and included a 1960's picture of the lieutenant governor wearing long hair, a beard and tie-dyed clothing. Because the ad began airing so close to Election Day, Scranton was unable to respond to it. When the dust cleared, Casey was elected governor by a margin of about 79,000 votes.

Casey was inaugurated on January, 20, 1987. Casey called for an "activist government," and he favored expanding health care for women, reforming the welfare system, educational opportunities and environmental improvements. In his first budget he gave legislators a $12,000 raise, and he also raised his own salary. Despite the fact that he had raised their salary, his relationship with the state lawmakers was not a smooth one. At one point he publicly chided the legislature for their inaction on programs he favored. As detailed in John Baer's aforementioned book on one occasion Casey invited some legislators to the Governor's mansion for cocktails in an attempt to better relations. He asked a lawmaker named Bob O'Donnell what the problem was. O'Donnell told Casey, "There are two kinds of Irish: those that breed the poets, the drunks and the politicians; and those that breed the priests. We are mostly the former. I'm afraid you, lad, are the latter."

Casey was known for his strong stand against abortion. In 1989, he succeeded in passing the "Pennsylvania Abortion Control Act" which placed limitations on abortions. Planned Parenthood filed suit naming Casey as the defendant. The case went all the way to the United States Supreme Court where in June of 1992, the court upheld all of Pennsylvania's abortion restrictions except one. In addition, the court affirmed the rights of states to restrict abortion.

In 1990, Casey was easily reelected beating Barbara Hafer who was Pennsylvania's Auditor General at the time. Hafer made headlines when she called Casey "a redneck Irishman." Hafer did correctly predict that the state would face a billion dollar deficit in 1991. As a result Casey's next budget included $2.86 billion in new taxes.

Since Casey felt that abortion would be an important issue in the 1992 presidential election, he wanted to make a speech at the Democratic National Convention on the issue. The convention managers refused to give him a speaking slot, and Casey complained that he was being censored due to his pro-life views. After the convention, Casey went on vacation, and many thought he did so to avoid campaigning for Bill Clinton.

Yet another example of how important Casey felt the abortion issue was occurred in 1991 when one of Pennsylvania's Republican Senators, John Heinz, was killed in a plane crash. As Governor, it was Casey's job to appoint someone to fill the vacancy. He settled on a former aid to President John F. Kennedy named Harris Wofford. Casey extracted two promises from Wofford before he made the appointment. First, when he ran to be elected to the office he would choose James Carville to manage the effort, and second on the issue of abortion Wofford would support the Pennsylvania Abortion Control Act. With those promises, Casey actively supported Wofford in the special election held that fall when he defeated former Pennsylvania Governor Richard Thornburgh. After that election, Casey urged Wofford to support a legislative amendment which was similar to the Pennsylvania law. Casey threatened to withdraw

Here is the grave of a man who finally won the office of Pennsylvania Governor by running under the slogan "The Real Bob Casey."

his support in the next election if Wofford went the other way. Wofford supported the amendment but was defeated anyway in the 1994 election by Rick Santorum. Casey's oldest son would take the seat from Santorum in the election of 2006.

Early in his second term Casey was diagnosed with hereditary amyloidosis. It's a rare disease that had just a few years before claimed the lives of Pittsburgh Mayor Richard Caliguiri and Erie Mayor Louis Tullio. Casey's condition was made public just a few days before he underwent a rare heart-liver transplant on June 14, 1993. As a result many felt that Casey had been given preferential treatment by being moved ahead of others who were on organ donor waiting lists. For any family that has ever had a family member on such a list, it would be difficult to come to a different conclusion. Today there is an organ donation trust fund named in his honor. After the transplants, Casey continued to suffer from the effects of the illness, and he passed away on May 30, 2000. He was laid to rest in Saint Catherine's Cemetery in Moscow, Pennsylvania.

If You Go:

Should you choose to visit Bob Casey at Saint Catherine's, there are a couple of other graves you may want to visit. **James Crowley** (See *Keystone Tombstones Volume 1*), one of the four horsemen of Notre Dame, is buried there, and so is **Patrick DeLac**y who was awarded a Congressional Medal of Honor. You are also in the vicinity of two other interesting cemeteries covered in *Keystone Tombstones Volume I* (See Chapter on Congressman **Dan Flood** and Chapter on **Mary Jo Kopechne**). In addition, the area has many other attractions including quality golf courses, a triple A minor league baseball team, a major concert venue, and more than a few fine dining establishments. We recommend a visit to Woodlands Inn and Conference Center. The Woodlands offers multiple bars and eating establishments. The rooms are reasonably priced. You may also want to look into their vacation packages.

Jim Crowley (College Football Hall of Fame)

Jimmy Dorsey

6.
A Fabulous Dorsey

Jimmy Dorsey
County: Schuylkill
Town: Shenandoah
Cemetery: Annunciation of The Blessed Virgin Cemetary
Address: Shenandoah Heights section

In American popular music, Jimmy and Tommy Dorsey achieved that all too rare combination: musical sophistication and vast commercial appeal. The Dorsey brothers were responsible for some of the most memorable music of the swing era. They consistently topped the charts with some of the best rhythms ever recorded. Born in Shenandoah, PA in 1904, James Francis Dorsey was the eldest of the two. Their father was a music teacher in the local high school and tutored the boys in their musical pursuits. He started playing the trumpet and switched to alto saxophone and then learned to double on clarinet. In 1920, he and Tommy, who played trombone, formed their own combo "Dorsey's Novelty Six," one of the first jazz bands to broadcast on the radio. Jimmy also played alone and in big bands and even in pit bands for Broadway musicals.

In 1930 he joined Ted Lewis's band for a tour of Europe. When he returned from Europe, he and his brother kept busy as studio musicians and occasionally co-led an orchestra backing some well-known singers including Bing Crosby. In 1934, they officially formed the Dorsey Brothers Orchestra that included the soon to be famous Glenn Miller. They started recording and soon had some impressive hits such as "I Believe in Miracles" and "Lullaby of Broadway." Many of their songs featured Bob Crosby (Bing's younger brother) on vocals.

Though the two brothers shared leadership, Tommy fronted the band and did most of the work. Jimmy was content to sit with the orchestra and was perfectly happy letting Tommy take charge. Tommy was well known for his temper. He had tremendous drive and often expected too much for those who worked for him. Tommy often resented Jimmy who was easy going and well-liked by the band members. Jimmy was everyone's pal, while Tommy was distant. One night in June 1935 tensions came to a head. Tommy counted off the tempo for their next number, and Jimmy interrupted him saying it was too fast. Tommy didn't say a word but grabbed his trombone and walked offstage, never to return. Everyone asked him to come back, but he refused. The Dorsey Brothers Orchestra became the Jimmy Dorsey Orchestra with vocalists Bob Eberly and Kay Weber. Jimmy Dorsey within a few years emerged as one of the top bandleaders of the day. His brother Tommy now had his own band and a recording contract with RCA Victor and also had a high level of success.

In 1939, Jimmy hired Helen O'Connell as his female singer. She and Bob Eberly projected a boy and girl next door charm, and their pairing produced several of the band's biggest hits. They had eleven number one hits in the 1930s and 1940s. His

In 1947 the Dorsey Brothers, both of whom led highly successful swing bands for more than a decade, sat for this publicity photo for The Fabulous Dorseys, a Hollywood film about their lives and careers. (Image Donated by Corbis-Bettmann)

biggest hit "Amapola" was number one for ten weeks in 1942 on the Billboard pop singles chart. Bing Crosby recorded "Pennies from Heaven" with the Jimmy Dorsey Orchestra, and it went number one for ten weeks and was one of the top records of 1936. In 1957 "So Rare" went as high as number two and was on the charts for 26 weeks. There were movies too. Jimmy Dorsey appeared in a number of Hollywood motion pictures including "That Girl from Paris," "Shall we Dance," "The Fleets In," "Lost in a Harem" with Abbot and Costello, "I Dood It" and "The Fabulous Dorseys."

Amid that string of vocal hits and movies, it's easy to forget that the Jimmy Dorsey band was also a serious jazz outfit, whose members liked to stretch out when they could and just play and leave the vocalist on the sidelines. How good was Jimmy Dorsey? The level of virtuosity he commanded on the alto sax or the clarinet was rated in the same league with Benny Goodman and Artie Shaw.

In 1947 Jimmy and Tommy began to reconcile while filming their quasi-biographical movie "The Fabulous Dorseys."

In 1953, Jimmy and Tommy reunited and formed a new band "Tommy Dorsey and his orchestra featuring Jimmy Dorsey." They gained a good deal of notice for their regular appearances on the Jackie Gleason Show which led to a weakly variety program "StageShow" hosted by the brothers on CBS from 1954-1956. Elvis Presley

This tombstone marks the final resting place for one of the "Fabulous Dorseys."

appeared on several of the telecasts, including his first appearance on national TV in January 1956.

Tommy died in 1956 at the age of fifty-one. He apparently choked to death in his sleep. He was apparently so sedated he didn't awaken when the choking began. Jimmy was devastated by his brother's death and did not outlive him for very long. He passed away seven months later on June 12, 1957 after a bout with cancer. He was 53. He is buried in the Annunciation of the Blessed Virgin Mary Church Cemetery beside his parents. Shortly before his death, he was awarded a gold record for "So Rare" which was recorded in November 1956.

On February 8, 1960 Jimmy Dorsey was inducted into the Hollywood Walk Of Fame. His star is on the North side of the 6500 block of Hollywood Boulevard

In 1983 Jimmy Dorsey was inducted into the Big Band and Jazz Hall of Fame. He is also a member of the American Jazz Hall of Fame. In 1996 the U.S. Postal Service issued a Jimmy Dorsey and Tommy Dorsey commemorative postage stamp, honoring them for their contributions to American music. The Jimmy Dorsey Orchestra has continued successfully for decades and is still in great demand all over the world.

If You Go:

Shenandoah is a small old coal mining town that is very hilly, and it feels like you've stepped back in time. It's the Kielbase Capital of the East Coast and home to Mrs. T's Pierogies. There is a state historical marker dedicated to the Dorsey brothers at Main and Center Streets in Shenandoah.

7.
40 Heroes

Flight 93 Crash Site
County: Somerset
Town: Shanksville
Address: 6424 Lincoln Highway

Just about every adult American remembers where he or she was on September 11, 2001. On that day, the deadliest terrorist attack in U.S. history took place when four commercial airliners were hijacked by members of the Islamic extremist group Al Queda. Two of those planes, American Airlines Flight 11 and United Airlines Flight 175, were crashed into the North and South towers, respectively, of the World Trade Center Complex in New York City. A third plane, American Airlines Flight 77, hit the western side of the Pentagon just outside Washington, D.C.

The nation's capital was also the target of the fourth plane, United Airlines Flight 93. Instead, it crashed into a field in Stonycreek Township, Pennsylvania, near

This monument marks the opening of the Flight 93 memorial.

Shanksville, after its passengers tried to overcome the hijackers. Nearly 3,000 people were killed during the attacks on September 11, a number that almost certainly would have been higher if not for the heroic actions of those aboard Flight 93.

Flight 93 was a regularly-scheduled nonstop flight from Newark, New Jersey, to San Francisco, California, set to depart at 8:00 a.m. The flight was delayed due to heavy air traffic and took off at 8:42 a.m. with 37 passengers and seven crew members. Four of the passengers were terrorists with plans to hijack the plane and fly it into the U.S. Capitol building. They had successfully boarded the plane with knives and boxcutters.

The hijacking began at 9:28 a.m., when the terrorists infiltrated the plane's cockpit. Air traffic controllers heard what they believed to be mayday calls and sounds of a struggle. At 9:32 a.m., a hijacker (later identified as Ziad Jarrah) was heard over the flight data recorder directing the passengers to sit down and stating that there was a bomb on board. The flight data recorder also shows that Jarrah reset the autopilot, turning the plane around and heading it towards Washington. By this time, the first two planes had already hit the World Trade Center in New York.

At 9:39 a.m., Jarrah once again announced that there was a bomb on board, that the plane was returning to the airport, and that the passengers should remain quiet. Air traffic controllers did not hear from the flight again.

The passengers began making calls using airphones and cell phones. A total of ten passengers and two crew members were able to complete phone calls. By now, the third plane had hit the Pentagon. Huddled in the back of the plane making calls and exchanging information, the passengers learned the fate of the three other hijacked flights, realized what was going on, and began to plan an insurrection.

One of the passengers, Tom Burnett, made several phone calls to his wife, Deena. He pumped her for information and interrupted her several times to tell the others what she was saying. During one of the calls, he told her:

"I know we're all going to die. There's three of us who are going to do something about it. I love you honey."

Another passenger, Todd Beamer, was heard by a GTE phone operator over an open line saying to his fellow passengers:

"Are you guys ready? Okay. Let's roll."

Flight attendant Sandra Bradshaw called her husband and told him she was preparing scalding water to throw on the hijackers. She ended by saying:

"Everyone is running up to first class. I've got to go. Bye."

At 9:57 a.m., the passengers and crew began their assault on the cockpit. Jarrah began to roll the aircraft left and right to knock the passengers off balance. The cockpit voice recorder captured sounds of crashing, screaming and the shattering of glass.

According to the 9/11 Commission Report, Jarrah and another hijacker discussed intentionally crashing the plane into the ground before the passengers could break through to the cockpit - even though such a move would obviously prevent the hijackers from destroying their intended target in Washington (which was still more than 150 miles away at that point). There were indications that the passengers were

This is a view of the actual crash site the remains of the victims are buried here.

using a food cart to ram the cockpit door. The plane headed down and rolled onto its back, at which point one of the hijackers can be heard on the voice recorder shouting "Allah is great! Allah is the greatest!" The Report concludes that the hijackers remained at the controls but must have judged that the passengers were only seconds from overcoming them. With the sounds of the counter-attack continuing, the aircraft plowed into an empty field in Shanksville ... about 20 minutes flying time from the U.S. Capitol.

Flight 93 fragmented violently upon impact. All human remains were found within a 70-acre area surrounding the impact point. By December 21, 2001, all of the people on board the flight had been identified. Investigators were not able to determine if any of the victims were dead before the plane crashed. It was later revealed that on the day of the crash, two F-16 fighter jets from the 121st Fighter Squadron of the D.C. Air National Guard had been scrambled and ordered to intercept Flight 93. Since time constraints at take-off had prevented the pilots from being able to arm their jets with missiles, their plan - had they reached Flight 93 - was to ram the Boeing 757's cockpit and tail areas (hopefully ejecting from their respective jets just prior to impact).

Although the details of what happened on board Flight 93 will never be fully known, all 40 passengers (not counting the hijackers) and crew are recognized as heroes.

Two years after the attacks, federal officials formed the Flight 93 National Memorial Advisory Commission responsible for making design recommendations for a permanent memorial. A temporary memorial had been formed from spontaneous tributes left at the crash site by visitors in the days and weeks after the attacks. The first phase of the permanent memorial was dedicated on September 10, 2011, the day before the 10th

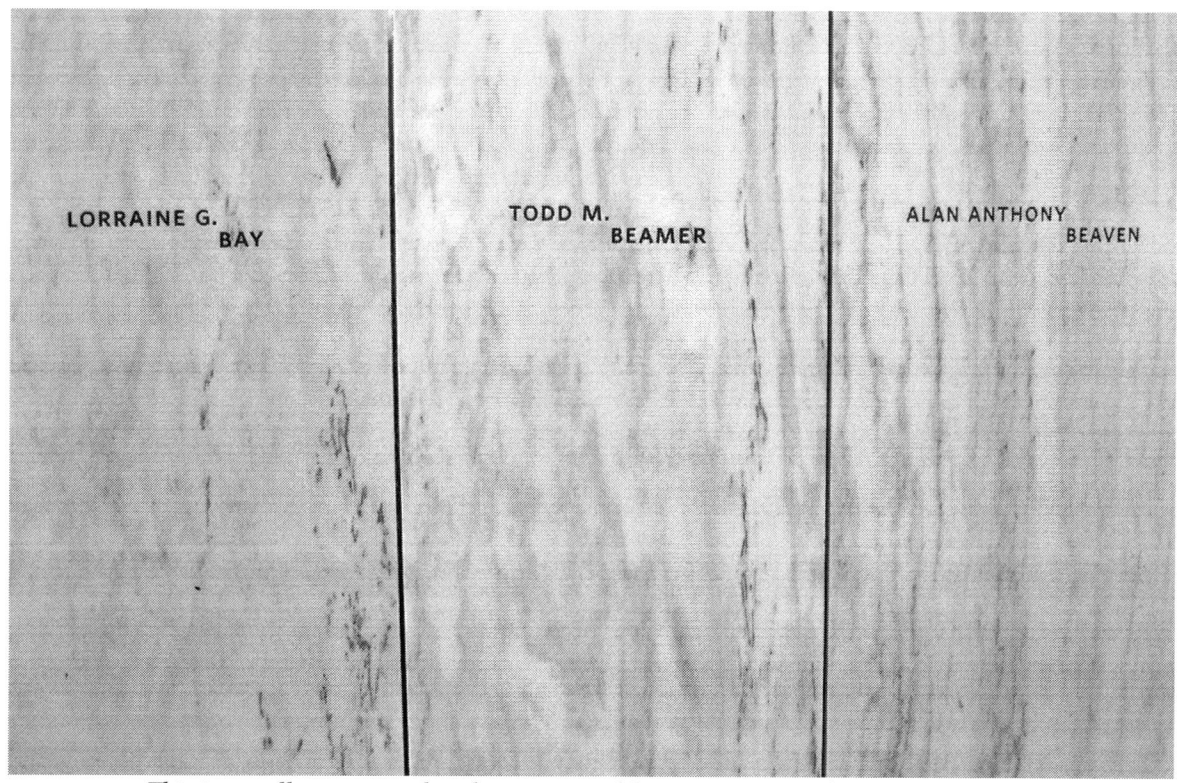

This is a wall constructed to the memory of the passengers and crew on the flight.

anniversary of the crash. On September 11, 2012, the remains of those killed were buried in a private ceremony for family members and police, fire and emergency workers who had responded to the scene exactly 11 years earlier. The remains, which had been kept in three caskets in a crypt for 10 years, were placed to rest after being looked after by Somerset County Coroner Wallace Miller.

The National Park Foundation has received over $40 million for the memorial from more than 110,000 individuals, foundations and corporations. The funds have already been used to build the new park's Memorial Plaza, Wall of Names, 40 Memorial Groves and the Field of Honor. A new visitors' center is expected to open in 2015, which will contain a permanent collection of artifacts and a learning center.

At the National September 11 Memorial in New York, the names of the 40 victims of Flight 93 are inscribed on Panels S-67 and S-68 at the South Pool.

In April 2012, the United States Navy launched a newly-constructed warship which it dubbed the *USS Somerset*. The name honors the passengers of Flight 93. Flight 93 has also been the subject of various films and documentaries, including the 2006 Hollywood feature film *United 93*.

THE 40 HEROES OF FLIGHT 93
THE CREW & PASSENGERS

Crew Members:	Age:	Hometown:
Captain		
Jason M. Dahl	43	Littleton, Colorado
First Officer		
LeRoy Homer	36	Marlton, New Jersey
Flight Attendants		
Lorraine G. Bay	37	East Windsor, New Jersey
Sandy Waugh Bradshaw	38	Greensboro, North Carolina
Wanda Anita Green	49	Oakland, CA & Linden, NJ
CeeCee Ross Lyles	33	Fort Pierce, Florida
Deborah Jacobs Welsh	49	New York City, New York

Passengers:	Age:	Hometown:
Christian Adams	37	Biebelsheim, Rheinland-Pfalz, Germany
Todd M. Beamer	32	Cranbury, New Jersey
Alan Anthony Beaven	48	Oakland, California
Mark Bingham	31	San Francisco, California
Deora Frances Bodley	20	San Diego, California
Marion R. Britton	53	Brooklyn, New York
Thomas E. Burnett, Jr.	38	Bloomington, Minnesota
William Joseph Cashman	60	West New York, New Jersey
Georgine Rose Corrigan	55	Honolulu, Hawaii
Patricia Cushing	69	Bayonne, New Jersey
Joseph DeLuca	52	Succasunna, New Jersey
Patrick Joseph Driscoll	70	Manalapan, New Jersey
Edward Porter Felt	41	Matawan, New Jersey
Jane C. Folger	73	Bayonne, New Jersey
Colleen L. Fraser	51	Elizabeth, New Jersey
Andrew (Sonny) Garcia	62	Portola Valley, California
Jeremy Logan Glick	31	Hewitt, New Jersey
Kristin White Gould	65	New York City, New York
Lauren Catuzzi Grandcolas and Unborn Child	38	San Rafael, California
Donald Freeman Greene	52	Greenwich, Connecticut
Linda Gronlund	46	Greenwood Lake, New York
Richard Guadagno	38	Eureka, CA & Trenton, NJ
Toshiya Kuge	20	Osaka, Japan
Hilda Marcin	79	Mount Olive, New Jersey
Waleska Martinez	37	Jersey City, New Jersey

Nicole Carol Miller	21	San Jose, California
Louis J. Nacke, II	42	New Hope, Pennsylvania
Donald Arthur Peterson	66	Spring Lake, New Jersey
Jean Hoadley Peterson	55	Spring Lake, New Jersey
Mark David Rothenberg	52	Scotch Plains, New Jersey
Christine Ann Snyder	32	Kailua, Hawaii
John Talignani	74	Staten Island, New York
Honor Elizabeth Wainio	27	Baltimore, Maryland

If You Go:

The Flight 93 crash site is in a very remote location. However, if you do decide to make that trek then we recommend you also pay a visit to the **Quecreek Mine Rescue site**, located in Lincoln Township not far from the crash site. It was there in 2002 that nine miners were trapped underground for over 78 hours. In an amazing rescue that unfolded before a live national television audience over the course of several days (July 24-28), all nine miners were saved and eventually made full recoveries.

A memorial park is located at the farm field just west of Route 985 where the drilling operations to rescue the miners took place. Driving directions and other helpful information may be found at http://www.quecreekrescue.org. There is a bronze statue of a miner at the park's entrance, and at the rescue site itself you will find the "Monument for Life" - a plaque mounted to a large boulder which sits in front of a red oak tree surrounded by nine pine trees. This dramatic rescue operation has inspired books and movies and is a testament to the human spirit.

Joseph Hewes

8.
Four Founders

Joseph Hewes
Francis Hopkinson
George Ross
Benjamin Rush
County: Philadelphia
Town: Philadelphia
Cemetery: Christ Church Burial Ground
Address: 5th and Arch Streets

They were all American Patriots who risked all for their country. They were all signers of the Declaration of Independence. They all contributed to the American victory during the Revolution. Joseph Hewes amassed a fortune in the shipping business in Wilmington, North Carolina. Francis Hopkinson was from New Jersey and made a name for himself as a lawyer, judge, composer, poet and satirist. George Ross served as a colonel in the Continental Army and as judge of the Admiralty Court of Pennsylvania. Benjamin Rush was a physician who is known as the father of American psychiatry. In addition he was a professor of chemistry and a social reformer. What they all had in common was a firm belief that America required independence.

Joseph Hewes was born in Princeton, New Jersey, on January 23, 1730. His parents were Quakers, a religion Hewes would eventually renounce. Hewes attended Princeton University, but there is no evidence that he ever graduated. As a young man he became an apprentice of a very successful merchant. His work as an apprentice earned him the respect of others and a strong reputation. At the age of thirty he moved to North Carolina where the people grew to like and respect him as a result of his honesty in conducting business. In 1763, after living in North Carolina for just three years, he was elected to the state legislature. During this time he amassed a fortune in the shipping business.

By 1773, a majority of the people living in North Carolina favored independence. Hewes was elected to represent the colony as a representative to the Continental Congress in 1774. Unlike the people of his state, Hewes did not favor independence; he was convinced that reconciliation with England was possible. Hewes attempted to bring representatives from other states around to his view with little success. As a result he threw himself into his work. He worked on numerous committees and ironically most that he served on favored independence.

By 1776, Hewes had already sacrificed quite a bit for his country. For two years Congress had been pushing for a system of nonimportation in order to hurt the English economy, but the idea had gone nowhere. Hewes worked with some of his counterparts and together they formed a nonimportation association. Belonging to such an

Francis Hopkinson

organization was costly for Hewes as a huge chunk of his business involved English imports.

By the summer of 1776, it was obvious the Congress was going to declare independence. On July 1,1776,as John Adams argued for independence Hewes said, "It is done! I will abide by it." Hewes signed the Declaration of Independece.

Hewes put his ships at the new country's disposal to use as they saw fit. Hewes had a friend by the name of John Paul Jones. Through Hewes, Jones obtained a navy commander's assignment. Jones would become the United State's first navel hero. Hewes would serve as Secretary of the Navel Affairs Committee until 1779 and as a result he could be considered the "Father of the U. S. Navy." Hewes returned to North Carlina to settle business and private affairs.

He returned to Philadelphia in 1779, where he fell ill on October 29,1779. He died on November 10th and was laid to rest at the Christ Church Burial Ground. Before his death, he described himself as a sad and lonely man. The woman he loved died a few days before their wedding, and he never married. As a result there were no children to inherit his money and estates.

Francis Hopkinson was born in Philadelphia on October 2, 1737. He was a member of the first class of the College of Philadelphia (now the University of Pennsylvania) when he was 14. He graduated in 1757, and received a master's degree in 1760.That same year he began the study of law with Benjamin Chew and in 1761, he was admitted to the bar. Hopkinson's first significant position was secretary to the Pennsylvania Indian Commission in 1761, where he assisted in developing a treaty with the Delaware and Iroquois Indian tribes.

Hopkinson was an author and songwriter. He wrote political satires in the form of poems and pamphlets. When he was 17 he began studying the harpsichord. He is said to be the first American composer to write a composition and put it on paper with his 1759 work "My Days Have Been So Wondrous Free." Hopkinson also played the organ at Christ Church in Philadelphia. In the 1780"s he modified a harmonica which was to be played with a keyboard and invented an instrument called the Bellarmonic. In 1778 he published eight songs for his friend George Washington

Hopkinson made his living in the dry goods business. He was married in 1768, and he and his wife had 5 children. He moved to New Jersey in 1774. In 1775 he was sent to represent New Jersey in the Second Continental Congress, and as a member of Congress he signed the Declaration of Independence. He left Congress in November of 1776 in order to serve on the navel board of Philadelphia. He was appointed judge of the Admiralty Court of Pennsylvania in 1779, and he aided in the ratification of the United States Constitution in 1787. In 1789 President George Washington nominated Hopkinson to be the judge of the United States District Court for the District of Pennsylvania. The United States Senate confirmed the nomination. Only a few years into serving in this position Hopkinson died in Philadelphia from a sudden epileptic seizure. He was 53 years old. He is buried in the Christ Church Burial Ground. At one point Hopkinson claimed that he had designed the American flag, and he asked Congress for a bottle of wine for his efforts. Congress denied the claim so now every year on his birthday, the workers at Crist Church take a bottle of wine to his grave in remembrance of his contribution.

George Ross

George Ross was born in New Castle, Delaware in 1730. He was named after his father who was a minister who presided over the local Episcopal church. As a young man he was educated at home. When he was 18, as was the norm for the times, he took up the study of law at a brother's law office in Philadelphia. He was admitted to the bar and with his sympathies at the time leaning toward England he became the Crown Prosecutor for 12 years and in 1768 he was elected to the provincial legislature. It was during this time that his feelings toward England began to change and he soon became a strong supporter of the various colonial assemblies in their disputes with Parliament.

In 1774 he was selected to be one of Pennsylvania's delegates at the 2nd Continental Congress. As a member he became a signer of the Declaration of Independence. In 1776, he became a Colonel in the Continental Army. That same year he acted as Vice President of the State constitutional convention where he helped write a declaration of rights. He was re-elected to Congress in 1777 but due to poor health he resigned that position that same year. In 1778 he began service acting as an admiralty judge and in 1779 he became Judge of the Admiralty Court of Pennsylvania. That same year he died in office and was buried in Christ Church Burial Ground in Philadelphia.

Benjamin Rush was born on January 4, 1746, in Byberry, Pennsylvania. His family included seven children and when Rush's father died it was up to his mother to care for the large family. Rush was five at the time. When he was eight Rush's mother sent him to live with an aunt and uncle in Maryland. His uncle, Samuel Finley, ran a private school and he was instrumental in convincing Rush to become a doctor.

In 1760, Rush graduated with a Bachelor of Arts degree from the college of New Jersey which is now Princeton University. In 1761 he began an apprenticeship under a Doctor John Redman in Philadelphia. Redman convinced Rush to continue his medical studies at the University of Edinburgh in Scotland. He graduated in 1768 with a medical degree.

Rush returned to America in 1769 at the age of 24. He opened a medical practice in Philadelphia and became a professor of chemistry at the College of Philadelphia which is now the University of Pennsylvania. He would eventually publish the first American chemistry textbook.

Around this time Rush joined the Sons of Liberty and began writing essays in favor of American independence. As a result of these activities Rush was appointed to the Second Continental Congress in 1776. While serving in Congress he became a signer of the Declaration of Independence.

Rush was instrumental in encouraging Thomas Paine to publish "Common Sense." As a matter of fact Rush came up with the title. Rush was always worried about his reputation in Philadelphia and was therefore very happy that he had found someone else to pen such an anti-English essay.

Rush became surgeon general of the middle department of the Continental Army in 1777. In this capacity he clashed with Dr. William Shipman who was the director general of hospitals for the army. Rush believed that Shipman was responsible for the miserable health conditions the army faced. He filed a formal complaint against Shipman, but Congress investigated and found the complaint to be without merit.

In 1778, Rush made a mistake he would regret for the rest of his life. He sided with a group whose aim was to remove George Washington as commander in chief. Rush

Benjamin Rush

Keystone Tombstones – Volume 3

This stone marks the grave of an American patriot and a signer of the Declaration of Independence.

This is the grave of a man who fought in the Continental Army after signing the Declaration of Independence.

Here is the final resting place of Benjamin Rush a signer of the Declaration of Independence whose many other achievements are largely unrecognized.

This is the grave of Francis Hopkinson a talented musician and composer who also signed the Declaration of Independence.

sent an unsigned letter to Patrick Henry urging Washington's removal. Though the letter was unsigned Rush was easily identified as the author due to his distinctive handwriting style. Rush was left with no choice but to resign from the army.

Rush returned to a very busy civilian life. In 1783, he was appointed to the staff of the Pennsylvania Hospital. Next he was elected to the convention to be held in Pennsylvania that would ratify the United States Constitution on December 12, 1787. In 1791, he became professor of medical history and clinical practice at the University of Pennsylvania.

Rush's accomplishments include the establishment of Dickinson College in Carlisle, Pennsylvania as week as the Philadelphia Society for Alleviating the Miseries of Public Prisons and served as the treasurer of the U.S. Mint. He also acted as the intermediary in providing the reconciliation between John Adams and Thomas Jefferson.

In 1793 Philadelphia was hit by an outbreak of yellow fever. Rush was one of three doctor's available to treat the more than 6,000 people affected by the fever. He worked, often without proper rest, to halt the epidemic. Eventually he developed a new and improved treatment by combining calomel and jalap. This combination aided in curbing the spread of the fever.

Rush died in 1813 from an unspecified illness. He was laid to rest in the Christ Church Burial Ground.

If You Go:

The Christ Church Burial Ground charges a modest entrance fee. The money raised is used to cover the cemeteries maintenance costs. The man the authors consider the first American Benjamin Franklin (See *Keystone Tombstones Volume 1*) is buried here along with a number of other important Americans. If you make the trip you are in the midst of Philadelphia's historic district. Independence Hall, the Constitution Center and the Betsy Ross House are within easy walking distance. In addition there are numerous restaurants in the area should you desire refreshments.

9.
Fox and Cox

Nellie Fox
County: Franklin
Town: Saint Thomas
Cemetery: Saint Thomas Town Cemetery

Billie Cox
County: Perry
Town: Newport
Cemetery: Newport Cemetery
Address: 1125 Middle Ridge

South Central Pennsylvania is the final resting place for two baseball greats; Nellie Fox and Billy Cox.

Jacob Nelson Fox was born on Christmas day, 1927 in St. Thomas Township Pennsylvania near Chambersburg. His father, Jake, earned his living as a carpenter and played second base on the St. Thomas town team. As a boy Nelson was often called "Pug." He wasn't called Nellie until he began his professional baseball career. Fox loved baseball and started out as the batboy for the town team. He eventually joined his dad on the town team and played first base. He played ball almost everywhere he could find a team: on the St. Thomas High School team, in The American Legion League, and in the nearby Chambersburg Twilight League. As a teenager he took up chewing tobacco which would become one of his trademarks.

The young Fox was never much of a student. He was frequently caught reading sports books or magazines when he was supposed to be doing school work. His mother, Mae, was concerned about his future and in early 1944 she wrote to Philadelphia Athletics Manager Connie Mack (See *Keystone Tombstones Volume One*, Chapter 16) for advice. She explained that he was "baseball crazy," "won't study" and talks constantly about Mack and the Athletics. Mack wrote a nice letter back saying that it was possible to make a living playing ball.

World War II created a lot of openings in professional baseball, and this made young Nellie think he might have a shot despite his small size and young age of 16. In the spring of 1944, encouraged by Mack's letter, he convinced his father to take him for a tryout to Frederick, Maryland where the Philadelphia Athletics were training. Mack liked Fox's determination and signed him to a contract to play for Lancaster in the Pennsylvania Interstate League.

Two years later in 1946 his contract was purchased by Philadelphia, but Fox spent the entire season in military service in Korea. He got brief call ups from the minors in 1947 and 1948 and spent all of 1949 with the Athletics but was a backup player. A few weeks after the 1949 season ended, he was traded to the Chicago White Sox and his career took off. He spent 14 seasons with the White Sox and two with Houston. He was selected twelve times as an All Star, won three Gold Glove Awards and was the league's Most Valuable Player in 1959. The 1959 season was Fox's best, and he led the White Sox to their first pennant in 40 years. He hit .306, had an on-base average of .380 and won the Golden Glove award. In the World Series, which they lost to the Dodgers in six games, he batted .375. He led the league in hits four times, in games

Nellie Fox

played five times and in singles seven years in a row. Being only 5'9" and about 155 pounds, he hit only 35 home runs, but using a thick handled bat and spraying hits to all fields he batted over .300 six times, had 2,663 hits and was one of the toughest batters to strike out. He led the league in most at-bats per strikeout 13 times. He struck out once every 42.7 at-bats which ranks him third of all time. He was also known for using the smallest fielder's glove available throughout his career, so as to "feel the ball" better and serve to smooth the transitions to throwing for the completion of double plays. He and Luis Aparicio were a formidable double play combo from 1956 to 1962. Bronze Statues of each of them are on the outfield concourse of U.S. Cellular Field, the White Sox home field. His uniform number 2 was retired by the White Sox.

After his playing career, Fox was a coach for the Houston Astros (1965-1967) and the Washington Senators/Texas Rangers (1968-1972). He retired from baseball in 1972, returned to St. Thomas and operated a bowling center, Nellie Fox Bowl, in nearby Chambersburg. It still operates today.

In 1975, Fox was diagnosed with lymphatic cancer. His decline was slow and agonizing. He died in Baltimore on December 1, 1975, twenty four days before what would have been his 48th birthday. Washington manager, Jim Lemon, said the cancer, "had to be incurable because if it wasn't Nellie would've beat it." In 1997 he was inducted into the Baseball Hall of Fame. All-time great New York Yankee pitcher Whitey Ford had this to say about Fox: "Nellie was the toughest out for me. In twelve years I struck him out once, and I think the umpire blew the call."

Nellie Fox is buried in St. Thomas Town Cemetery in Franklin County. His well-kept grave is marked with a large stone that has his picture in a Texas Rangers uniform and many of his accomplishments etched on the stone.

William Richard "Billy" Cox was born on August 29, 1919 in Newport, Pennsylvania where he was an exceptional high school baseball player for Newport High School. He graduated in 1939 and played shortstop for the Newport semi-pro team. In 1940 he was signed by the Harrisburg Senators, a Pittsburgh Pirate farm club of the Interstate League, where he hit well and was an all-star shortstop. In 1941 he led the interstate league in batting, hits, doubles and total bases for Harrisburg. His average was .368 and included a 22 game hitting streak. His performance was noticed and he was called up to the Pirates in September and played in 10 games hitting .270. It was a promising start that would unfortunately be delayed four years by war. Billy Cox entered the U.S. Army shortly after the attack on Pearl Harbor. He was initially stationed at the nearby New Cumberland Reception Center with the 1301St Service Unit. In May 1942 a very unusual thing happened. The Pittsburgh Pirates were playing an exhibition game against the Harrisburg Senators and by special permission of the Army, Cox was able to play with the Pirates for that night against his former team mates. "The appearance of Private Billy Cox in the line-up for the Pittsburgh Pirates was the magnet for a crowd of nearly 3,500 fans" wrote the Sporting News. Cox was soon assigned to the 814th Signal Corps and saw action in North Africa, Sicily, Italy, France and Germany. He was discharged as a Corporal in November 1945 at Indiantown Gap Separation Center and within days married his high school sweetheart, Anna Radle.

Although he had missed four seasons and was now 26, he wasn't resentful. He felt lucky he said to go "through four years of war and came out whole". After two good seasons with the Pirates he was traded to the Brooklyn Dodgers. The Dodgers moved

Billy Cox

Here is the modest grave of the great Brooklyn Dodger third baseman Billy Cox.

him to third base and he played there for seven seasons and three National League Championships. He played with one of the greatest infields ever, that included Gil Hodges, Jackie Robinson and Pee Wee Reese. During the 1953 World Series Casey Stengel said of him "That ain't a third baseman. That's a f------g acrobat." He was known for taking his glove off between every pitch and having a cannon for an arm; he

Nellie's tombstone is a testament to his greatness on the diamond.

Billy Cox Memorial Field in Newport, Perry County, PA.

had the habit of looking at the ball in his throwing hand for just an instant before he fired the ball to the appropriate base.

After the 1954 season, Cox was traded to the Baltimore Orioles and then in mid-season to the Cleveland Indians. He refused to report to Cleveland and went home to Newport instead.

Billy Cox is featured prominently in Roger Kahn's widely-acclaimed book *The Boys of Summer* and is also a prominent character in Carl Erskine's *Tales from the Dodger Dugout: Extra Innings*.

He died in Polyclinic Hospital in Harrisburg of esophageal cancer on March 30, 1978 at the age of 58. He is buried in a very modest grave in Newport Cemetery in Newport, PA.

If You Go:

We paid a visit to Billy Cox Memorial Field, a youth baseball park on North Second Street in Newport. The Newport Hotel and Tavern also on North Second Street is a good place to have a drink and a bite to eat and reflect and discuss baseball history, or just history, or just baseball, or the weather or ...

10.
Smokin' Joe

Joe William Frazier
County: Philadelphia
Town: Philadelphia
Cemetery: Ivy Hill Cemetery
Address: 1201 Easton Road

He was considered one of the greatest heavyweight boxers of all time. His three fights with Muhammad Ali have achieved legendary status. Howard Cosell's repeated cries of "down goes Frazier" during his fight with George Foreman is cemented as one of the greatest sportscasting performances of all time. He was known to boxing fans as "Smokin' Joe" Frazier.

Joseph William Frazier was born on January 12, 1944, in Beaufort, South Carolina. He was the 12th child born to his parents. His early life was lived on the ten acres of farmland owned by his family. In later years Frazier recalled that he was particularly close to his father who would carry him to the still where he made bootleg liquor. Frazier's parents worked the farm which had very poor soil. All they were able to grow was cotton and watermelon.

In the early 1950's Frazier's parents purchased a television. Frazier's family would get together and watch boxing matches. Frazier viewed bouts that featured fighters like Sugar Ray Robinson and Rocky Marciano. During this period one of Frazier's uncles, after taking note of his nephew's sturdy build said, "that boy is going to be another Joe Louis." The next day Frazier constructed his own heavyweight bag that for years he worked on almost every day. It's clear that by this time Frazier's toughness was already in evidence. His classmates would pay him a quarter to walk home with them so the bullies would leave them alone.

At the age of 15 Frazier found work on a farm owned by a white family named Bellamy. One of the Bellamy's was a tough man named Jim. One day a 12 year old black boy accidentally damaged a tractor on the farm. Jim was so angry that he used his belt to whip the boy. Frazier witnessed the beating, and he told other black workers on the farm what he had seen. Later Jim Bellamy confronted Frazier and demanded to know why he told the other workers. Frazier denied he had done so, but Bellamy didn't believe him, and he threatened to take off his belt again. Frazier told Bellamy that he wasn't going to use that belt on him. Bellamy sized up Frazier and decided to settle things by telling Frazier to get off his farm. After this incident Frazier decided he had to leave Beaufort. He took a bus to New York where he lived with one his brothers.

Frazier then began his amateur boxing career. In 1962, 1963 and 1964 he won the Golden Gloves Championship in the heavy weight division. In the three years he fought as an amateur, he only suffered one loss and that was to Buster Mathis. In 1964 Frazier attempted to make the United States Olympic Boxing team. He fought his way

Joe Frazier

to the final of the Olympic Trial where he was matched up against none other than Buster Mathis. Frazier was out to revenge his only loss, but at the end of the bout the judges declared Mathis the winner. Frazier disagreed with the judges and remarked, "all that fat boy had done was run like a thief, hit me with a peck and backpedal like crazy." The loss depressed Frazier, and he actually thought about giving up boxing. Fortunately his trainer, Yank Durham, talked him out of it and even convinced Frazier to go as an alternate to Tokyo where the Olympics would be held.

The decision to go to Tokyo turned out to be a good one. Mathis was injured, and Frazier replaced him on the American team. He won his first two fights by knock out. He was the only American boxer left entering the semi-finals. His next opponent was Vadim Yemelyanov from the Soviet Union. Yemelvanov was 6 foot 4 and weighed 230 pounds. Frazier was pounding the Russian and knocked him to the canvas twice in the second round. Late in that round, Frazier landed a left hook and felt a jolt of pain shoot through his arm. He had broken his thumb. Fortunately for Frazier the match was decided in his favor when Yemelvanov's corner men threw in the towel.

Frazier was determined to fight in the final, so he kept the news of his broken thumb to himself. His opponent in the final was Hans Huber who was representing Germany. Frazier relied mainly on his right hand during the bout. He threw very few left hooks, and his punches were not as powerful as they had been in his previous fights. After three rounds it was up to the five judges to decide the winner. Three of them voted for Frazier making him the gold medal winner. Frazier was the only United States boxer to win an Olympic gold medal.

Following the Olympics, Frazier turned professional in 1965. He won his first fight when he knocked out Woody Goss in the first round. After that he won three successive fights, and no opponent lasted longer than three rounds. Then during training Frazier's left eye was badly injured, so badly that he was declared legally blind in that eye. Somehow Frazier continued to pass pre-fight physicals in spite of this condition. Frazier then fought Mike Bruce who actually sent Frazier to the canvas in the first round. Frazier beat the referee's count and knocked Bruce out in the third round.

It was about this time in 1966 that Frazier's trainer, Yancey Durham, convinced Eddie Futch to join Frazier's team as an assistant trainer. Futch was centered in Los Angeles so Frazier went there to train. Frazier fought three times on the west coast winning all three bouts. One of the fights was against George Johnson who went a full ten rounds with Frazier before losing a decision. Ring magazine reported that Johnson bet his entire purse that Frazier would not knock him out.

In 1967 Muhammad Ali was stripped of his heavyweight title when he refused to be inducted into the military. A heavyweight elimination tournament was set up to crown a new champion. At the time Frazier was the number one contender but Futch convinced him to not participate in the tournament. Fitch was also instrumental in Frazier adopting a bob and weave style which made it more difficult for his opponents to land their punches. At the conclusion of the tournament Jimmy Ellis was crowned Heavyweight Champion.

On February 16, 1970, Frazier fought Ellis at Madison Square Garden for the undisputed heavyweight title. Ellis had never been floored in his career, but Frazier sent him to the canvas twice in the fourth round. When the bell sounded to start round five, Ellis remained in his corner, and Frazier was the new Heavyweight Champion.

Joe Frazier landing one on Muhammad Ali

    In his first bout defending his title Frazier, who had won 26 straight fights, went up against the Light Heavyweight Champion Bob Foster. In the second round, Frazier sent Foster to the floor twice. The second knockdown came as a result of a powerful left hook, and Foster was unable to beat the count. This successful defense set up what would be called the "fight of the century" when Frazier would meet Muhammad Ali who was back in boxing after a three year suspension.

    The fight took place in Madison Square Garden on March 8, 1971. Both Ali and Frazier were undefeated, and Ali as usual was predicting a victory. Once again Eddie Futch was a major factor in the outcome of the bout. Futch noticed that Ali had a tendency to drop his right hand prior to using it to deliver a powerful punch, and he instructed Frazier to watch that hand and when he saw it drop to deliver a left hook to Ali's face. Ali won many of the early rounds, but then Frazier began coming on and began pounding Ali to the body. In the 15th round Frazier saw Ali drop his right hand and Frazier, as instructed, delivered a left hook that sent Ali to the canvas. Frazier was declared the winner by unanimous decision. The contest saw both fighters head to the hospital afterward, and Frazier remained there for a week.

After defeating Ali, Frazier successfully defended his title against Ron Stander and Terry Daniels. Though he had won both fights, many observers felt that he hadn't been as dominant as he had been in previous bouts. In his next title defense Frazier was matched against George Foreman. Although Frazier was the favorite, there were boxing experts, including Howard Cosell on hand to broadcast the event, who were picking Foreman to win. Regardless of predictions nobody expected the fight to unfold the way it did. Frazier came out fast and landed his patented and powerful left hook, but it failed to faze Foreman. It could be that right then Frazier knew he was in trouble. The challenger responded with a combination followed by a right uppercut that sent the champion down. Howard Cosell screamed three times in a row "down goes Frazier." The moment is still remembered as one of Cosell's finest moments.

Frazier rose from the canvas only to be floored again before the round ended. Early in round two Foreman again connected with a right that sent Frazier to the canvas. Cosell described it as target practice for Foreman. Foreman didn't let up, and he floored Frazier three more times. After the 6th knockdown, the referee stopped the fight, and Foreman was the new champion.

Frazier continued to fight winning his next two bouts which set up a rematch with Ali. The fight was considered a letdown based on their earlier bout because there were numerous clinches. After 12 rounds, Ali was declared the winner though many disputed the decision. By the time Frazier

Beautiful grave site of the great heavyweight champ Smokin' Joe Frazier. (& the reflection of the photographer -- Joe Farley)

and Ali would meet again, Ali would be the champion based on the fact that he knocked out George Foreman in 1974.

It can be argued that the third Ali – Frazier fight was the greatest heavyweight championship bout of all time. It took place on October 1, 1975 in the Philippines and became known as the "Thrilla in Manila." Before the fight Ali consistently referred to Frazier as "The Gorilla." From the beginning, the fight was intense and punishing. Early in the bout Ali said to Frazier, "They said you were through Joe." Frazier responded, "They lied, pretty boy." After the 14th round Frazier's eyes were swollen shut, and Eddie Futch refused to let him answer the bell for the final round. Ali

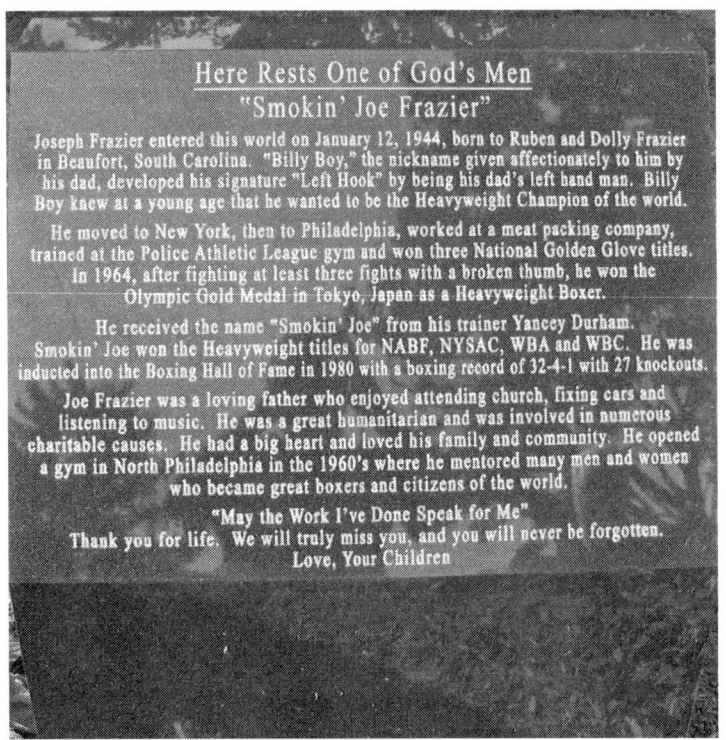

Monument at the grave of Smokin' Joe.

emerged the winner, but he commented later that the fight was the "Closet thing to dying that I know of."

Frazier fought a few more bouts before announcing his retirement. He made a brief comeback in 1981 fighting one time before he retired for good. His final record as a professional was 32 wins, 4 losses and 1 draw.

In his later years, Frazier lived in Philadelphia where he owned and managed a boxing gym. He and Ali continued their rivalry. When Ali lit the Olympic flame in 1996, Frazier said that he would have liked to have thrown Ali into the fire. It wasn't until 2009 that Frazier said he no longer had bad feelings about Ali. Frazier was diagnosed with liver cancer in September of 2011. He died on November 7th of that year. Ali was among those who attended his funeral.

If You Go:

Others buried in Ivy Hill Cemetery include **Willie Anderson**, **Franklin Gowen** and **Bill Tilden**. Anderson was the first golfer four U.S. Open Championships (see *Keystone Tombstones,* Chapter 1). Gowen was famous for leading the prosecution, some would say persecution, of the Molly Maguires in the 1870's (see *Keystone Tombstones Volume One,* Chapter 21). Tilden was a tennis great who dominated that sport in the 1920's and 30's (see *Keystone Tombstones Volume One,* Chapter 27). Both **Harold Melvin** of Harold Melvin and the Blue Notes and **Marion Williams** the famed gospel singer are also buried at Ivy Hill, but they are in unmarked graves. You can still visit their gravesites as the folks working in the cemetery office will be glad to provide you with their locations. In addition if you are at Ivy Hill, you are about a mile away from Holy Sepulcher Cemetery. **Frank Rizzo** and **Connie Mack** are buried there. Rizzo was a colorful and controversial Mayor of Philadelphia (see *Keystone Tombstones Volume One,* Chapter 25). Mack was a legendary major league baseball manager (see *Keystone Tombstones Volume One,* Chapter 16).

11.
The Communicator

Dave Garroway
County: Montgomery
Town: Bala Cynwyd
Cemetery: West Laurel Hill
Address: 215 Belmont Avenue

Dave Garroway was a broadcast pioneer. He was the original host of the morning television program "Today" on NBC television. The first show to combine news and entertainment, "Today" was considered a brash experiment when it premiered in 1952.

David Cunningham Garroway was born in Schenectady, New York on July 13, 1913. His family moved many times before eventually settling in St. Louis, Missouri, when Dave was 14. He attended University City High School and Washington University in St. Louis, where he earned a degree in psychology.

After graduation in 1935, Garroway tried his hand as a lab assistant at Harvard, and then as a salesman (selling books initially, and then later piston rings - neither successfully). He decided to take a stab at broadcasting after he made it through the highly competitive interview process to land a position as a page at NBC. The page program gave young people a temporary job at Radio City in New York and later the NBC Studios in Hollywood. NBC's pages would work in various departments at the network, being groomed for a career with NBC. In addition, the pages acted as ushers and tour guides. Only 60-80 pages were selected from thousands of applicants each year, one of whom in 1938 was Dave Garroway.

Garroway got off to a rather mediocre start by graduating 23rd of 24 in his class at the NBC announcer school in 1939. Nevertheless, he landed a job at influential Pittsburgh radio station KDKA and built a reputation as the station's "Roving Announcer." He roamed the region filing a number of memorable reports from both above and below the Earth's surface (aboard a hot-air balloon and from deep within a coal mine, respectively) as well as underwater (aboard a U.S. Navy submarine in the Ohio River). This experience brought out Garroway's ability to find a compelling story in any situation. He soon became the station's special events director.

After two years at KDKA, Garroway left Pittsburgh for a job in Chicago. However, his career in broadcasting was interrupted in 1941 by the outbreak of World War II. He enlisted in the Navy and was stationed in Honolulu. When he was off duty, he hosted a radio show, playing jazz and reminiscing about Chicago.

After the war, he returned to Chicago and worked as a disc jockey at WMAQ (AM). He hosted a variety of programs and promoted the Chicago jazz scene. One of his innovations was to convince his studio audience to show approval for a song by snapping their fingers instead of clapping, just like the "hepcats" did in the coffee shops. He was voted the nation's best disc jockey in the Billboard polls in 1948, 1949 and 1951.

Farrell and Farley

Dave Garroway, "Peace"

Garroway broke into television when he hosted the experimental musical variety show "Garroway at Large," which was telecast live from Chicago. The show ran from 1949 to 1954 on NBC. He abandoned the usual conventions for a more casual approach and personal, informal style. In 1951, he came to the attention of legendary NBC president Pat Weaver, who recruited Garroway to host a new morning news-and-entertainment experiment called the "Today" show. The show debuted on January 14, 1952 and the critics initially panned it, but Garroway's laid-back style attracted a large audience that enjoyed his easygoing presence early in the morning.

On "Today," Garroway - who wore bowties and horn-rimmed glasses - was officially called "a communicator," and his former colleagues say the term was especially apt. His signature sign-off at the end of each broadcast was an upraised hand (palm out) saying "Peace." Barbara Walters, who Garroway hired to be a writer on "Today," said of Garroway, "I have never seen anyone in this business who could communicate the way he could. He could look at the camera and make you feel that he was talking only with you."

Garroway's co-host was a cute chimpanzee named J. Fred Muggs, and Garroway took the show to Paris and Rome, to car shows and expos, to plays and movies, and even on board an Air Force B-52 for a practice bombing run.

Garroway was a hard worker. At the same time he did "Today," he hosted a Friday night variety series called "The Dave Garroway Show," which ran from 1953 to June 1954. In 1955, he began hosting NBC's Sunday afternoon live documentary, "Wide Wide World," which ran until 1958. The premiere episode - featuring entertainment from the U.S., Canada and Mexico - was the first international North American telecast in the history of the medium. He also hosted a radio show, "Dial Dave Garroway," that went on the air as soon as the "Today" show wrapped up each morning, and for those who couldn't get enough of him there was a board game called "Dave Garroway's Today Game," which debuted in 1960.

Despite his easygoing camera presence, Garroway frequently battled depression. After his second wife, Pamela Wilde, committed suicide via drug overdose in April 1961, his condition worsened. A month later he resigned and on June 16, 1961, he hosted his last "Today."

After leaving the show, Garroway tried his hand at educational television (a series called "Exploring the Universe"), a return to radio, and even started a magazine. He studied acting (landing a role in an episode of the western series "Alias Smith and Jones" in 1972), narrated a compilation of songs performed by the Boston Pops Orchestra, and wrote a book (*Fun on Wheels*) to amuse children on road trips. He appeared sporadically on various television programs but never again achieved the success or recognition he enjoyed on "Today." He appeared on "Today" anniversary shows in the 60's and 70's; his final appearance was on the 30th anniversary show on January 14, 1982.

He had many interests and hobbies, such as restoring classic cars, astronomy, music and auto racing. He appeared in television commercials for the first Corvette in 1953 and the Ford Falcon in 1964. His interest in astronomy led him to his third wife, Sarah Lee Lippincott, an astronomer whom he married in 1980.

In 1982, Dave Garroway had open heart surgery. Various postoperative complications soon followed. On July 21, 1982, he was found dead of a self-inflicted gunshot wound at his home in Swarthmore, Pennsylvania. He was 69 years old.

Here is the grave of the broadcast pioneer Dave Garroway.

The Hollywood Walk of Fame honored Dave Garroway with a star at 6264 Hollywood Boulevard for his contributions to television, and another, separate star at 6355 Hollywood Boulevard for his contributions to radio. Because of his dedication to the cause of mental health, his third wife, Sarah, helped establish the Dave Garroway Laboratory for the Study of Depression at the University of Pennsylvania. He is buried in West Laurel Hill Cemetery in Bala Cynwyd.

If You Go:

West Laurel Hill is a beautiful, large cemetery, containing the graves of many famous and interesting people, several of whom are identified in Chapter 19 (Teddy Pendergrass) of this volume. Some others are:

William Breyer (1828-1882), the founder of Breyer's Ice Cream;

Hobart "Hobey" Baker (1892-1918), the Hall-of-Fame hockey player and World War I hero;

Robert Cooper Grier (1794-1870), a United States Supreme Court Justice, Grier was plucked from relative obscurity in August 1846 and nominated for appointment to the nation's highest bench by President James K. Polk, but not until *after* one of Polk's first nominees (fellow Pennsylvanian and future President of the United States, James Buchanan) refused the appointment; and

Herman Haupt (1817-1904), a very important Civil War general (*see Keystone Tombstones: The Civil War*, Chapter 25).

12.
The Human Windmill

Harry Greb
County: Allegheny
Town: Pittsburgh
Cemetery: Calvary Cemetery
Address: 718 Hazelwood Avenue

Harry Greb of Pittsburgh, Pennsylvania may have been the greatest fighter, pound-for-pound, who ever lived. At his peak he was unbeatable, defeating virtually every middleweight, light heavyweight and heavyweight of his generation.

Nicknamed the "Human Windmill" because of his perpetual motion style, he fought 299 official fights in 14 years - an average of nearly 21½ fights a year - against the best opposition the talent rich 1910's and 1920's could provide him. He fought everybody who was somebody in a golden era of teeming talent. He defeated 18 men who held, had held or would hold world championships. He defeated nine middleweight champions, eight light heavyweight world champions and one world heavyweight champion, Gene Tunney. Between winning the middleweight championship from Johnny Wilson in 1923 and losing it to Tiger Flowers in 1926, Greb defended his title six times and engaged in a total of 56 fights.

Born Edward Henry Greb on June 6, 1894 in Pittsburgh, he began his professional boxing career in 1913. Two years later he was fighting world class opposition such as Hall of Famer Tommy Gibbons and the reigning middleweight champ, George Chip. Greb would lose both fights by "newspaper" decision, losses he would later avenge. A "newspaper" decision is unheard of these days but was common during the early part of the 1900's. At that time, either by law or by prearrangement, if both fighters were still standing at the fight's conclusion and there was no knockout, no official decision was rendered and neither boxer was declared the winner. However, this did not prevent the ringside reporters from declaring a consensus result among themselves and printing it in their publications.

Greb fought a record 37 times in 1917 and won 34 of them either officially or by newspaper decision. Among his victims that year was the reigning light heavyweight champion Battling Levinsky, former light heavyweight champion Jack Dillon, middleweight George Chip and heavyweight Willie Meehan, who had beaten future champ Jack Dempsey earlier that year. Despite all these great results, Greb was denied a chance to fight for a title. In the span of just over a year (August 1918-September 1919) he fought and beat the reigning light heavyweight champ Battling Levinsky five times.

Greb married his childhood sweetheart, Mildred Riley, in 1917, and a year later they had a daughter, Dorothy, on whom he doted. Mildred was reportedly very beautiful and won a beauty pageant that years later became the Miss America Pageant. She had been a chorus girl at a burlesque theater on Liberty Avenue in Pittsburgh.

Harry Greb

Greb was shattered by his wife's death from tuberculosis in 1920. Greb's sister, Ida, and her husband, Elmer Edwards, adopted Dorothy some years later.

In 1919, Greb fought in 45 bouts, breaking his own record for most fights in one year. At his peak, he weighed between 158 and 165 pounds and stood 5'8" tall. He often fought men who outweighed him by as much as 40 to 80 pounds. In Greb's nearly 300 fights, he was unable to finish only twice: once in his first year of professional fighting; and once in 1915 when he broke his arm punching Kid Graves and was unable to continue.

In 1920, Jack Dempsey fought Billy Miske for the heavyweight championship. In preparation, Dempsey scheduled six sparring sessions with Harry Greb. The first three were in July at Dempsey's New York City training camp at Broadway and 57th Street. More than 2,000 fans paid to see the first of those on July 27. The *Pittsburgh Post* reported that in the third sparring match on July 29, Greb tore into the champion and time had to be called when Greb split open Dempsey's eye with a hard right in the second round. The *Post* said that Dempsey did not want to lose face so he continued the match briefly, but then he called it off for the day.

They sparred again on September 1, 1915, in Benton Harbor, Michigan, just five days before Dempsey's fight with Fiske (which Dempsey went on to win, retaining his world heavyweight title). Greb weighed 165 pounds and Dempsey weighed 190. The *New York Times* reported that Greb gave the champion a real, honest-to-goodness battle:

Greb was all over him and kept forcing him around the ring throughout the session. Dempsey could do but little with the speedy light heavyweight, while Greb seemed to be able to hit Dempsey almost at will.

The next day the two sparred for three rounds. In the third round, Greb's head collided with Dempsey's mouth, and he spat blood for the remainder of the round. On day three, the two fighters staged a whirlwind three rounds in front of over 2,000 people that burst into cheers and prolonged applause in appreciation of the furious action they were witnessing. Dempsey said that Greb was "the fastest fighter I ever saw."

In 1921, during a fight with tough light heavyweight Kid Norfolk, Greb was thumbed in the right eye and suffered a detached retina, which would ultimately leave him permanently blind in that eye. Greb fought on and knocked out Norfolk in the 11th round. He kept the injured eye and subsequent blindness a secret from all but his wife and closest friends for the remainder of his career (nearly five years) before eventually consenting to its removal in a private operation in Atlantic City. A perfectly matching glass eye was substituted, attached to the eye muscles by sheep tendons.

On May 23, 1922, Harry Greb finally got his title shot against Gene Tunney at Madison Square Garden. It would be the first of five fights between the two. Tunney was the undefeated American light heavyweight champion (the world title belonged to Frenchman Georges Carpentier). At the end of 15 rounds, Tunney was a bloody mess and Greb was the champion. The *New York Times* called Greb a "human perpetual motion machine" and the famous sportswriter Grantland Rice wrote "Harry handled Gene like a butcher hammering a Swiss steak. How Gene survived 15 rounds I will never know." It was the only official defeat of Gene Tunney's career.

After defending his title against Tommy Loughran, Greb granted Tunney a rematch. It resulted in an extremely controversial split decision that gave Tunney back the crown. Some writers called for an investigation of the decision, and many called it the

Here is the grave site of the boxer who was known to all as the "Human Windmill."

worst decision in New York history. The State Athletic Commissioner, the legendary William Muldoon, called the verdict "unjust" and declared that Greb should have received the decision.

Greb and Tunney would fight three more times, and they were all good, closely contested matches. The third time they met in the ring, Tunney won. The fourth bout was declared a draw despite two of three Cleveland newspapers calling it for Greb and the third calling it a draw. The fifth fight was won by Tunney in a 10-round decision. Greb suffered two broken ribs in the third round of that match. Afterwards, Greb acknowledged that Tunney was the better fighter, and the two became good friends. Tunney would go on to beat Jack Dempsey for the world heavyweight title in September 1926.

One month after losing his American light heavyweight title, Greb won the world middleweight title by defeating Johnny Wilson. Greb would defend the title four times, most notably in 1925 at the Polo Grounds against welterweight champion Mickey Walker. The *New York Times* reported:

Greb retained his world middleweight title when he battered his way to the decision . . . in as savage and furious a ring encounter as either boxer has ever experienced. Walker left the ring badly used up. He had a split lip, a bruised and battered nose, and a cut under his right eye which was puffed and almost closed. Greb was unmarked.

In 1926, Greb was past his prime when he lost his world middleweight title to Tiger Flowers in a split decision. Six months later, Greb lost a rematch to Flowers in another controversial split decision. Fans stormed the ring and threw anything they could lay their hands on in protest.

It was to be Greb's last fight. Two months later, he checked into a clinic in Atlantic City for surgery to repair damage to his nose and respiratory tract caused by his ring career and several car accidents. Complications ensued, and he died on October 22, 1926, at the age of 32, never regaining consciousness. Gene Tunney was among the pallbearers at his funeral. He is buried in Calvary Cemetery in Pittsburgh.

Harry Greb was the ultimate aggressive, swarming-style fighter. His perpetual motion style made him as dominant as any fighter who ever lived, and his awesome record (264-23-12) is virtually unmatched in the annals of boxing history.

If You Go:

Calvary Cemetery is a large, beautiful cemetery with many interesting graves. *Keystone Tombstones: Volume One* has chapters on **Harry Stuhldreher** (one of the legendary "Four Horsemen" of Notre Dame), **Frank Gorshin** (who portrayed the Riddler in the original "Batman" television series) and **David L. Lawrence** (considered "Pittsburgh's Renaissance Man" after serving an unprecedented four terms as that city's mayor before going on to become Pennsylvania's 37th Governor), all of whom are buried in Calvary Cemetery. Major league baseball's first 300-game winner and Hall of Famer member **James "Pud" Galvin** is also buried in a very modest grave at Calvary.

Pud Galvin

John Hartranft

13.
Old Johnny

John Frederick Hartranft
County: Montgomery
Town: Norristown
Cemetery: Montgomery Cemetery
Address: 1 Hartranft Avenue

John Frederick Hartranft was a union Major General and recipient of the Congressional Medal of Honor. He also served as Pennsylvania's Auditor General and then two terms as Governor from 1873 to 1879.

Hartranft was born in Fagleysville which is a village in New Hanover Township in Montgomery County Pennsylvania on December 16, 1830. He received a degree in civil engineering from Union College in Schenectady, New York in 1853 and worked for two railroads in eastern Pennsylvania before returning to Norristown to work with his father's real estate and stagecoach businesses.

In the spring of 1861 his militia outfit became a 90-day volunteer regiment and were sent to Washington D.C. On the eve of the First Battle of Bull Run, the regiment turned its back on the enemy and marched home just as the firing began. Their 90-day enlistment period was over and despite pleas for them to stay from General Irvin McDowell, they left. Hartranft was humiliated by his men's decision and he stayed to fight on July 21, 1861. This act earned him the Medal of Honor.

After Bull Run, he raised the 51st Pennsylvanian Infantry, a three year regiment, and became its colonel. They first served on the North Carolina coast in the Burnside Expedition and then at the Battle of Roanoke Island and New Bern. In 1862 they fought in the Second Battle of Bull Run and at South Mountain. On September 17, 1862 at Antietan, Hartranft led the 51st in its famous charge across Burnside's Bridge, suffering 120 casualties. They braved a storm of rifle and cannon fire to cross the bridge and threaten the Confederate right flank. They also participated in the Battle of Fredericksburg before being transferred to the Western Theater where Hartranft saw action at the battles of Vicksburg, Campbells Station and Knoxville. He fought at the Wilderness and at Spotsylvania after which he was promoted to brigadier general. After continuing to lead his forces against Richmond and Petersburg, he helped repulse General Robert E. Lee's last offensive at the Battle of Fort Stedman on March 25, 1865. His role at Fort Stedman led to him being brevetted major general by U.S. Grant.

The end of the war did not end the violence and death in Hartranft's life. President Andrew Johnson appointed him the provost marshal during the trial of those accused in the Lincoln assassination. The accused were being held in the Arsenal Penitentiary in Washington D.C. and he was responsible for the defense of the Arsenal as well as the supervision of every aspect of the prisoner's daily lives. He would make sure they were fed and cleaned and that no one would communicate with them unless authorized by Secretary of War Stanton.

"Destruction of the Union Depot" by M.B. Leiser, shows burning of Union Depot, Pittsburgh, PA during Great railroad strike of 1877 from pgs. 624, 625 of "Harper's Weekly, Journal of Civilization," Vol XXL, No. 1076, New York, Saturday, August 11, 1877.

    He also saw to it that the inmates were never allowed to occupy adjacent cells so as to prevent tapping out messages through the walls. The guard detail was changed on a daily basis to make sure that no single guard would guard the same prisoner more than once. On July 7, 1865 General Hartranft completed his duties by seeing to it that the sentence of Death for four of the prisoners was carried out. Hartranft led Mary Suratt, Lewis Paine, David Herold and George Atzerodt to the gallows in what is now called Fort Lesley McNair. They had received the news of their sentence only 24 hours earlier. One by one the conspirators were assisted up the thirteen steps of the scaffold by the execution party and seated. All four sat quietly while Hartranft publicly read the Orders of Execution, a five page hand-written document stating the charges against each of the four prisoners and the sentences of death that they received. Prayers followed and then the prisoners were told to stand and were positioned on the traps that would be knocked out from under them. Their arms and legs were bound, nooses were fitted around the necks and canvas hoods placed over their heads. From the scaffold Powell said "Mrs. Surratt is innocent. She doesn't deserve to die with the rest of us". Surratt would be the first women ever executed by the Federal Government. The signal was given by Hartranft and the condemned fell. Surratt and Atzerodt appeared to die quickly. Herold and Powell struggled for nearly five minutes, strangling to death.

Shortly after, Hartranft decided to end his military career. "Old Johnny" as his troops called him resigned from the army and decided to enter politics. He switched from the Democratic to the Republican party and gained the support of Republican state boss Simon Cameron (See *Keystone Tombstones Volume 1*) who recognized the voter appeal of his war record. He ran successfully for state auditor General in 1866 and again in 1869.

In 1872 he was Cameron's personal choice to succeed another Civil War hero John Geary (See *Keystone Tombstones Volume 1*) as governor and he won and served two terms until 1879. In contrast to Governor Geary, Hartranft had no objection to the expanding influence of the Pennsylvania Railroad and other industrial interests.

During his administration the revision of the Commonwealth's Constitution was completed and ratified as the Constitution of 1873. He played an important role in celebrating our nation's centennial in 1876 that was centered in Philadelphia's Fairmount Park. At the Republican National Convention in June 1876 he was a contender for the presidential nomination that eventually went to Rutherford B. Hayes of Ohio. Hartranft's second term was marred by economic depression, unemployment, strikes and civil unrest. He permitted the execution of twenty one coal miners convicted of various crimes in the coal region in North East Pennsylvania. Called the Molly Maguires, these men were leaders of labor unrest in the coal region. Ten of them were hanged in one day in Pottsville and Mauch Chunk on June 21, 1877 (See *Keystone Tombstones Volume 1*) The "King of the Mollies," Jack Kehoe, was also executed on December 18, 1878 after another extremely controversial prosecution in which coal company employees conducted the investigation, arrested Kehoe and then prosecuted him. Hartranft reportedly hesitated to implement the sentence explaining that he thought Kehoe should be punished but not hanged. Yet he waited until after the fall election and then signed a death warrant with one month left in his term. In July 1877 a series of riots broke out triggered by wage cuts for railroad workers. The worst riots were in Pittsburgh and Hartranft sent state militia and National Guard troops to maintain order. When outraged protesters cornered troops in a Pennsylvania Railroad roundhouse the soldiers opened fire, killing twenty and wounding many more. In response, furious workers destroyed tracks, roundhouses, engines and other railroad property. Protests spread to Altoona and Reading where National Guard troops killed another ten people.

Hartranft's obelisk

General Winfield Scott Hancock

As the violence spread to Philadelphia, Hartranft asked for (and received) federal troops from President Hayes, making him the first governor in U.S. history to request federal troops to put down a labor uprising.

In 1877, when 78-year-old Simon Cameron resigned his Senate seat, Hartranft appointed Donald Cameron - the Senator's son - to replace him. After leaving office, Hartranft returned to his home in Montgomery County and accepted the position of Postmaster. He later was appointed Collector of the Philadelphia Port.

John Hartranft died in Norristown on October 17, 1889. He is buried in a large grave marked by a large obelisk in Montgomery Cemetery, near Norristown. The Pennsylvania National Guard provided the obelisk for his grave. Ten years after his death, a heroic bronze, mounted statue of him was dedicated on the grounds of the Pennsylvania State Capitol in Harrisburg.

Marble monuments at Petersburg and Vicksburg honor his Civil War service. Elementary schools in Norristown and Philadelphia are named after the governor, as is a residence hall at Penn State University. There are streets named after him in South Philadelphia and in the Brookline section of Pittsburgh, and three avenues in Montgomery County are named in his honor. His Medal of Honor is commemorated by a stone bearing his name in Soldiers' and Sailors' Grove behind the State Capitol Building in Harrisburg.

If You Go:

There are a number of interesting Civil War graves in Montgomery Cemetery. There are Generals **Winfield Scott Hancock** (See *Keystone Tombstones Volume 2*) and **Samuel Kosciuszko Zook** (See *Keystone Tomb-stones Civil War*). Also buried there is **General Matthew McClennan** who led his troops in battles in the Richmond Campaign and **Edwin Schall** who served as Lt. Colonel of the 51st Pennsylvania and was killed at the Battle of Cold Harbor in June 1864.

Congressional Medal of Honor recipient **Hillary Beyer** is buried in a neigh-boring cemetery, and Brother Paul's is a great place to eat nearby.

14.
Much More than just a Scientist

Robert (Bob) Hess
County: Lancaster
Town: Elizabethtown
Cemetery: West Green Tree Church of the Brethren Cemetery
Address: 740 Green Tree Road

He was born, the second of four sons, on a farm near the small town of Mount Joy on June 9, 1928. From an early age he wanted to be a scientist. Instead he became a minister, a missionary, a professor, an administrator, a scholar, a writer, an aviator and a caring and loving husband and father. His gifts were many, and he shared of them freely. His name was Robert Hess.

Hess' early life was that of most of the farm boys of his time. He had his daily chores to attend to as well as his schoolwork. His grade school days were spent in a one room schoolhouse that held grades 1-8. This may have been an advantage for Hess in that being exposed to the work the older kids were doing probably helped hold his interest. As a matter of fact he skipped a year. His grades during this period were good though not exceptional. After his chores and schoolwork were completed he enjoyed playing with his three brothers. He particularly liked playing practical jokes on his older brother Wilbur.

1945 was a big year for Hess. First he graduated from Mount Joy High School where he received the Rotary Vocational Industrial Arts Award. In his yearbook the prediction for his future was that he would become a farmer (way off, though he did find a way to get his hands dirty in his adult years). Then in August of 1945 The United States dropped two atomic bombs on Japan. This proved to be a life changing experience for Hess who began thinking that maybe the world had enough scientists. As a result he began to rethink what he wanted to do with his future.

It was about this time that Hess approached a friend who regularly attended a prayer meeting and the next one was to be held that night. Hess asked his friend if he could accompany him to the meeting, and the friend said of course. Now the friend was a little surprised at Hess' request as he hadn't shown interest in the meetings before. Later on the way to the meeting Hess said, "You know I think I'm going to start dating Anna Mary Hawthorne. Since Hawthorne regularly attended the meetings the friend had discovered the source of Hess' sudden interest in the prayer meeting.

Soon Hess would begin his undergraduate studies at Elizabethtown College. He had also made good on his plan to begin dating Hawthorne, and the romance blossomed. Hess and Hawthorne were married on July 3, 1949, and one year later he graduated from Elizabethtown with a Bachelor's degree.

Having made the decision as to what he wanted to do with his life, he pursued his goals. In 1950 he was licensed as a minister in the Church of the Brethren. Hess and his wife then entered Bethany Biblical Seminary (now the Bethany Theology Seminary)

Bob Hess

where the two graduated in 1953. Hess had earned a Master of Divinity degree. The couple then chose the Nigerian mission field as their first place of permanent service.

Hess and his wife were initially assigned to Garkida where he temporarily directed the maintenance and building program. He did the same type of work at the Waka Schools Biu, as he honed his administrative skills. He was, however, a hands on administrator. The couple's next assignment was to a remote village at Wandali where they were the only foreign staff. Hess's duties included supervising the local primary school and medical dispensary as well as keeping the mission station property in repair. In addition he would visit other villages in the area to promote the growth of the church. By all accounts he was well liked and respected by the villagers who were grateful for his assistance. In 1955, while Hess was at Wandali, his only child was born, a girl that the couple named Sharon.

Due to the fact that there was a shortage of teachers at the Waka Teacher Training College, the family was transferred to Waka in 1956. By the following year Hess had been named principal of the training college. As a representative of the Church of the Brethren Mission, he applied for and obtained approval from the Government of Nigeria to open the first co-educational secondary school in that region. At that point he was named Superintendent of the Waka schools, a position he would hold until he retired from the Mission in 1969. During this period of time on one of the family's infrequent returns to the states he earned a Master of Education Degree from Temple University.

In spite of how busy he was with his duties he made sure that he found the time to spend with his wife and daughter. He would load Sharon on his motorcycle and ride her through the paths in the area until they ran out of gas. He would then tip the cycle to get the gas that remained in the bi-valve tank to where it needed to be to start the machine. He had the route so well planned that father and daughter always made it back to Waka riding the motorcycle.

Returning to the states he began teaching history and African studies at Messiah College. At the same time he was pursuing his doctorate degree at Howard University. He graduated in 1972 with a Doctor of Philosophy degree. Hess's responsibilities at Messiah continued to grow. He became the Coordinator of the Integrated Studies Program, a position he would hold until the program ended in the early 1990's. His teaching assignments grew as well as he would eventually teach African history, African culture, modern European history, anthropology, geography, Middle East History and computer applications for historians. After he retired in 1993, he continued teaching as an adjunct Emeritus Professor of History and African studies. It is impossible to gauge the effect he had on so many young lives during those years.

Meanwhile he was staying active in the Brethren Church. He was a member on the District board of the Atlantic Northeast District from 1972-77, 1979-84 and 1996-98. He was Chairman of that board for five years. He was also appointed to the Pennsylvania Commission for United Ministries in Higher Education and served as moderator for the West Green Tree

Hess with daughter Sharon

Church of the Brethren for fifteen years. In addition in 1997 he published a book titled "A People Committed The Story of the West Green Tree Church of the Brethren." In addition he was also instrumental in the development and publication of the "Hess Genealogy: the Descendents of 1717 Immigrants Hans and Magdalena Hess 1717-2004."

During this time Hess's wife Anna Mary remained busy raising their daughter and offering support wherever she thought it was needed. She was well known for her notes and letters of encouragement to family and friends, but her letter writing sometimes extended further. Mrs. Hess had been an exceptional athlete in high school and had a strong desire to stay in shape so she purchased an exercise bike that she rode regularly. In 2009 she decided to let the company who made the bike know how happy she was with it so she wrote the following letter to the Huffy Corporation on February 2nd:

Dear Sir/Madam
When checking some files lately I saw the manual of warranty for the Huffy exercise bike I have (model 90662). I can vouch for the fact that they are a sturdy bike. As of the above date I now have 39,280 miles on mine!! That represents about 30 years of biking and still going strong.
Anna Mary Hess
PS. In March I'll be 85 so I guess that gives me some bragging rights!

Huffy responded with a letter dated three days later:

Dear Anna Mary,
Thank you for such a nice letter about a product that Huffy made. We are no longer in the exercise business but it sure is nice to hear about your bike. I wish you more miles and happy riding on your bike. Hope you have a great birthday in March. I will pass your letter on to our Corporate Offices.

Final resting place of Robert Hess a man who proved to be more than just a scientist.

Huffy Bicycles Customer Service

Meanwhile, Hess while teaching and remaining active in the Church and pursuing his hobbies that included gardening for which he built a greenhouse, becoming a licensed pilot. But being a pilot wasn't enough, Hess decided he was going to build his own airplane and he did. Once when flying the plane the engine froze and he was forced to glide the plane down and land in a freshly plowed field. Local television crews were sent to the site to cover the story. Hess allowed the plane to be filmed but declined to be interviewed saying he hadn't done anything special. Later during an ice storm the roof of the hanger where Hess stored the plane collapsed destroying the aircraft. Arriving on the scene with a nephew to survey the damage Hess calmly said, "Looks like I'm going to have to build another plane." He did. As a pilot He was a member of the Experimental Aircraft Association from 1988 to 2003. He was also a member of the Smoketown Airport Chapter 540 until 2003 and found time to serve as the club's secretary for six years.

Hess passed away quietly on February 6, 2013. He touched the lives of many on two continents. Without a doubt his influence continues to be felt through those still with us who encountered him during his lifetime. Hess was laid to rest next to his wife in the West Green Tree Road Cemetery in Elizabethtown.

If You Go:

One place you can stop for refreshments is "Gus's Keystone family Restaurant" located at 1050 West main Street in Mount Joy. In addition you are very close to Lancaster where you can visit the graves of Pennsylvania's only President **James Buchanan** (See *Keystone Tombstones Volume 1*), a founding father **Thomas Mifflin** (also in Volume 1) and Congressman **Thaddeus Stevens** (See *Keystone Tombstones Volume 2*).

15.
The Kelayres Massacre

Joseph Bruno
County: Schuylkill
Town: McAdoo
Cemetery: Saint Patrick's Cemetery
Address: Lincoln Street

It was election eve in Schuylkill County Pennsylvania in the year 1934. Kline Township Democrats, expecting a big day at the polls in the morning, organized a parade. A local barber named Carl Vacante carried an American flag in front of the marchers who carried red torches. In addition vehicles carrying children were part of the parade. The marchers approached the home of Joseph Bruno a prominent Republican in the area. As they did some of the marchers began to chant "down with the Brunos." Suddenly shots rang out and five of the marchers were killed and many others were wounded. The incident became known as the Kelayres Massacre.

The Joseph Bruno family was active in real estate, bottling beer and politics dating back to the early 1890's. The family had members who held positions such as president of the school board, county detective, justice of the peace and inspector of weights and measures. Joseph Bruno's brother Philip was a tax collector, a Coal and Iron Policeman who also supplied various establishments with slot machines. By 1930 the Bruno family established political control over Kelayres.

Bruno used his position on the school board to enrich himself and his family. The schoolhouse in Kelayres burned to the ground under mysterious circumstances in 1932. The school board that Bruno controlled turned down an offer by a local coal company to rebuild the school. When construction on the new school began the trucks that were used were supplied by Bruno's brothers and Bruno himself acted as the purchasing agent. In that same year Bruno purchased the Lofty School for one dollar. He converted the building into a school bus garage, and the board agreed to rent the building for $30.00 a month.

Bruno was defeated in the school board election in 1933. However as justice of the peace he impounded the ballots and demanded a recount. Ballots were altered, and they favored Bruno. The controversy over the election led to Bruno's resignation but not before he arranged for his son Alfred to replace him.

Bruno's tenure on the school board was marked by corruption. Teachers were expected to give money to Bruno to keep their positions. By 1934 the teachers had formed a union to oppose the Brunos.

On election eve in 1934 the Brunos remained confident that they would prevail. The local democrats, equally as confident that the tide was turning in their favor, organized the fateful march. The purpose of the march was to signal the end of the 27 year long Republican rule that was headed by Bruno. Bruno family members occupied homes on

A parade turned into a bloodbath and became the Kelayres Massacre

two of the three corners at Center and Fourth streets and the democrats decided to March past those homes.

As the marchers approached the homes gunfire rang out. The gunfire came from both sides of the street causing the marchers to scatter in all directions. It was over in about a minute. Three people, William Forke 37, Frank Fiorella 65 and Joseph Galosky 30, died at the scene. Two others Dominic Perna, 37 and Andrew Kostician were rushed to a local hospital. Kostician died the following day, and he was wounded because upon hearing the shots he ran to the scene to search for his daughter. Perna died two days after being wounded. At a minimum 13 other marchers had been hit and required medical attention.

The initial calls to local police were ignored and believed to be prank calls because Bruno was well known and respected by the local authorities. When the police did make their way to Kelayres, they witnessed the carnage. They also found an angry mob planning to dynamite the Bruno household. When the police questioned Bruno and the other people in the house Bruno claimed to have heard shots and that they were aimed at his house. However when the police searched the house they found a shotgun, a pump gun, three doubled-barreled shotguns, three repeating rifles, automatic pistols and revolvers. In addition they discovered a dresser filled with ammunition. Bruno and six other members of his family were arrested.

The home of Joseph Bruno after the massacre.

In the election held the following day the Democrats swept the state. In Keylares out of 682 votes cast only 24 went to Republican candidates. Democrat George Earle was the first of his party to be elected Governor in decades. He along with a future Governor by the name of David Lawrence would attend the funeral for the five victims of the massacre. The funeral itself drew approximately 20,000 mourners. Many local businesses closed on the day of the funeral including banks, the post office, stores, schools and some of the local collieries. Five hearses took the bodies through the town of McAdoo to their final resting place. As the hearses passed them a number of women screamed in Italian "If you do not send those murderers to the electric chair, we will kill them ourselves."

At the trials the prosecutors produced witnesses who testified that the shots had come from the homes occupied by the Brunos. Witnesses for the defense claimed that the shots came from the home of Dan McAloose who was a local Democratic leader. At his initial trial Bruno was convicted of manslaughter. He appealed the verdict and received a second trial. At that trial Bruno was convicted and sentenced to life while his son Philip was sentenced to ten to twenty years. The other family members were acquitted. However at a third trial both Joseph and Philip were convicted of first degree murder while James, Arthur and Alfred Bruno were convicted of manslaughter.

Joseph Bruno had been convicted and sentenced to three life sentences. He was jailed in the Schuylkill County Prison in Pottsville. Two years later Bruno complained about a sore tooth. A prison guard was assigned to take Bruno to a doctor. Believe it or not when the guard couldn't find a parking place he told Bruno to get out of the car in front of the doctor's office and to wait for him there while he found a place to park. When he returned to the office Bruno was nowhere to be found.

About eight months later Bruno was found and apprehended living under an assumed name in New York City. He was returned to the Schuylkill County Prison

Joseph James Bruno

Here are the graves of Philip (left) and Joseph Bruno (right). Two men who were considered civic leaders yet opened fire on unarmed marchers killing five and wounding countless others.

where he served time for the next ten years until his sentence was commuted. All the others involved in the massacre had had their sentences commuted earlier in the 1940's. Bruno died in Kelayres of natural causes in 1951.

If You Go:

You are very near the center of Hazleton where you can visit a number of sites connected to the **Lattimer Massacre** (See *Keystone Tomstones Volume 2*) including a very sad scene of 14 of the victims of that massacre with their tombstones standing side by side at the Saint Stanislaus's Polish Catholic Cemetery located at 652 Carson Street. We also recommend a visit to the Battered Mug located on the corner of Beech and Pine Streets. We enjoyed the best pierogies we had ever tasted on our visit there. In addition you are close to a number of people we covered in *Keystone Tombstones Volume 1* including **Jack Kehoe** of the Molly Maguires and the man many consider to be the greatest athlete of all time, **Jim Thorpe**. If you visit Jim Thorpe we suggest a visit to the old jail which is now a museum where a number of the alleged Mollies were hanged. In addition you can't go wrong by visiting the Molly Maguire Pub where you will find good food and drink at reasonable prices. Finally the town of Jim Thorpe is very near the Pocono's, so depending on the season you can enjoy white water rafting or skiing.

16.
Golf's Unknown Champion

John McDermott
County: Delaware
Town: Yeadon
Cemetery: Holy Cross Cemetery
Address: 626 Baily Road

He remains the youngest player to ever win the United States Open Golf Championship. As a matter of fact he won it twice and in back to back years, 1911 and 1912. He was also the first American to win it and the first to break par. His name was John McDermott.

McDermott was born on August 12, 1891 in Philadelphia. His father was a mailman, but his grandfather owned a farm that was located across the road from the Old Aronimink Golf Club. It was during a visit to his grandfather's that he first learned about the game of golf. At the time he was under 10 years old.

McDermott became a caddy, and the pro at Aronimink, Walter Reynolds, took a liking to him and taught the young boy the game. As time went on, Reynolds helped McDermott land his first job as an assistant at a golf course in Camden County, New Jersey. He later moved to the Atlantic City Country Club. It was at this club where he developed his practice routine. McDermott would begin practicing at about 5AM every morning. He would hit shots for the next three hours. At 8AM he opened the pro shop and gave members golf lessons. He would conclude his day by playing a round himself. His routine became legendary.

In 1909, at the age of 17, McDermott played in his first U. S. Open. He finished 49th. Over the next year, McDermott's game improved dramatically. The 1910 Open was held at the Philadelphia Cricket Club Course. When the tournament concluded, McDermott was tied for the lead with two Scottish brothers MacDonald and Alex Smith. In the playoff Alex prevailed, but McDermott beat his brother MacDonald by two strokes.

By 1911 McDermott had developed a confidence in his game that he was willing to express publicly. With that year's U. S. Open approaching, he told other golfers in the Atlantic City locker room that the foreigners were through. He also told an assistant pro who had McDermott's clubs in tow that the assistant was carrying the clubs of the next Open champion.

The Open was held in Chicago, and once again after 72 holes McDermott found himself in a three- way playoff. This time he won the playoff by two strokes. In doing so he became the first American born Open winner and at 19 he was, and still is, the youngest to ever win the event. With McDermott's victory, the American public's interest in both the game of golf and the U. S. Open grew dramatically. It could be said that due to McDermott's victory Americans no longer viewed golf as strictly a European

Johnny McDermott. With the U.S. Open trophy. Won U.S. Open in 1911 & 1912

game. The great sportswriter Grantland Rice considered McDermott to be the greatest golfer America had ever produced.

In 1912 the Open was held at the Country Club of Buffalo. The field totaled 131 golfers which was the most ever at the time. McDermott prevailed again with a 72 hole score of 294 which included a final round where he shot 71. He had now won back to back Opens, and in doing so he also became the first player to score under par over 72 holes. Newspapers began comparing McDermott to the four time Open champion Willie Anderson (See *Keystone Tombstones Volume 1* Chapter 1).

In 1913 two great European golfers travelled to America to compete in the Open. One was Harry Vardon who had last come to the States in 1900 where he easily took home the Open Championship. The other was Ted Ray who was the British Open champion at the time. Both were expected to be McDermott's chief competitors at the Open.

The three met prior to the Open when they played in a tournament at Shawnee-on-the-Delaware. McDermott ran away from the field beating runner up Alex Smith by 8 strokes and Vardon by 13. After the victory McDermott's confidence got him into trouble when he proclaimed, "We hope our foreign visitors had a good time, but we don't think they did, and we are sure they won't win the National Open." Later McDermott apologized for the remark, but the press in both America and England continued to report it in their stories leading up to the Open. These stories increased public interest in the upcoming event.

The 1913 Open was played at the Country Club In Brookline, Massachusetts. Despite McDermott's claim Vardon was generally considered to be the favorite. After two rounds Vardon had a share of the lead with Ray two strokes behind. McDermott shot a 79 in the second round and found himself six strokes off the pace. At the end of 72 holes there was a three way tie at the top, but McDermott was not among the three as he finished in eighth place. Instead Vardon and Ray found themselves tied with a young American amateur by the name of Francis Quimet.

Heading into the playoff most considered it to be a match between Vardon and Ray. McDermott actually did play a role in the match in that he took Quimet aside and offered some advice. He told Quimet, "just play your own game, pay no attention to Vardon and Ray." In a stunning upset Quimet shot a 72 and beat Vardon by five strokes and Ray by six.

At this point McDermott ran into some bad luck. He had invested his winnings into stocks, and those investments had gone badly virtually erasing the money he had won as a professional golfer. In 1914 he sailed to England to participate in the British Open. However he missed both a ferry and a train and arrived at the course too late to qualify. Then as he was returning to America the ship he was on collided with another boat. McDermott was put into a life boat where he remained for twenty hours before being rescued. It was an experience that he was never able to put behind him.

First McDermott faced the public criticism after his comments about foreign players hit the press. This was followed by the failed effort to win his third open and his stock losses. This was followed by the shipwreck and combined they took a terrible toll on the young man. He entered the 1914 United States Open, but he displayed none of the confidence that had marked his personality. He finished in eighth place ten strokes behind the winner Walter Hagen.

In October of 1914, McDermott blacked out and collapsed at the Atlantic City Country club. His parents were notified, and he was returned home. That December

John McDermott

McDermott resigned his position at the Country Club. His father convinced him to enter a hospital, and he spent the rest of his life in institutions. At the age of 23 his professional golfing career was over.

There were times his family took him off the hospital grounds and he would play a round of golf. In addition a six hole course was built on the grounds of the Norristown Hospital, and he played there as well. Walter Hagen Vvsited McDermott in 1928 and played a round with him on the grounds.

McDermott's sister on occasion would take him to tournaments. At one event an assistant pro kicked McDermott out of the pro shop based on what the assistant considered strange behavior. The assistant couldn't believe it when one of the players in the tournament told him that he had just kicked out a two time winner of the U. S. Open.

McDermott was a spectator at the 1971 Open which was held in Ardmore, Pennsylvania. A golfer by the name of Arnold Palmer recognized McDermott and asked him how his game was. McDermott replied that he was hitting the ball well but was having trouble with his putting. Palmer put his arm around McDermott and said, "the only thing we can do is keep practicing."

That would prove to be McDermott's last Open. On August 1, 1971 the old golfer died in his sleep. He was close to eighty years old. He was buried at Holy Cross Cemetery in Yeadon, Pennsylvania. Some golf historians believe that, if not for his illness, he had the potential to be the greatest golfer of all time. McDermott's sister said that the only time she ever saw her brother cry was when he was informed that he had been inducted into the Golf Hall of Fame.

McDermott is portrayed in the movie "The Greatest Game Ever Played." The movie tells the story of Francis Quimet's upset victory in the 1913 Open. In one scene the

This tombstone marks the grave of the first native born American to win the United States Golf Open Championship.

actor playing McDermott issues a boastful challenge to other golfers in the clubhouse. The scene is based on the statements made by McDermott after the tournament at Shawnee.

If You Go:

Holy Cross Cemetery is large and well maintained with many interesting graves including America's first serial killer Dr. Henry Holmes and five members of the Philadelphia mafia (See *Keystone Tombstones Volume Two* Chapters 14 and 18 for those stories).

Louis van Zeist

Also buried at Holy Cross is **Louis Van Zeist** who was the bat boy and mascot for the Philadelphia Athletics from 1910 to 1914. Due to a childhood accident his growth was stunted, and he had a hunchback. He loved sports, and one day he went to Shibe Park and asked **Connie Mack** (See *Keystone Tombstones Volume One* Chapter 16) if he could be a bat boy. Mack took an instant liking to Van Zeist and gave him the job. In the early part of the 1900's hunchbacks were considered to be good luck, and players would rub the hump before going to bat. Van Zeist became a favorite of both the A's players and their fans, so in 1910 Mack hired him for all the home games and had a uniform made for him. It appears that he did bring the team some luck as the A's won their first world championship in 1910 and then repeated that feat in 1911 and 1913. In 1914 they won the American league title. In the winter of 1915 Van Zeist was diagnosed with Bright's disease, and he passed away in March. The Athletics didn't win another pennant until 1929.

There are four Congressional Medal of Honor recipients buried at Holy Cross. **William Shipman, George Crawford Platt** and **William Densmore** received their medals for bravery during the Civil War. **Philip Gaughan** received his for his conduct in the Spanish American War.

Frank Hardart of the famous Horn and Hardart restaurants was laid to rest in Holy Cross. The first restaurant opened in Philadelphia in 1902. Hot entrees, cold sandwiches, bowls of soup and slices of pie awaited behind the glass doors which opened when the right number of nickels were inserted. Hardart died in 1918.

The cemetery is also the final resting place for two Hall of Fame boxers. **Thomas Loughran** was a Light Heavyweight Champion who is considered to be one of the most skilled fighters of all time died in 1982. The other fighter is **Joseph Hagen** who was the Light Heavyweight Champ from 1905 to 1912. Hagen passed away in 1942.

17.
The Mysterious Case of Mary Pinchot Meyer

Mary Pinchot Meyer
County: Pike
Town: Milford
Cemetery: Milford Cemetery
Address: Route 209 – Milford

She was born on October 14, 1920, in New York City, to a wealthy and politically connected family. Her father was a lawyer active in the Progressive party who contributed funding to the socialist magazine "The Masses." Her mother was a journalist who wrote for magazines such as "The Nation" and "The New Republic." Her uncle Gifford Pinchot was a two time Governor of Pennsylvania (See *Keystone Tombstones Volume One* Chapter 22). She would eventually marry Cord Meyer who would go on to work for the Central Intelligence Agency. She would become a friend and lover of President John F. Kennedy. She was murdered in the fall of 1964, and many believe her death was related to her interest in the assassination of President Kennedy. Her name was Mary Pinchot Meyer.

Meyer grew up at the Pinchot family home named Grey Towers in Milford. As a child she met a number of left leaning intellectuals through her parents including Louis Brandeis and Harold Ickes. She was educated at Brearley School and Vassar College. It was during these years that she developed an interest in communism. This did not bother her father at all. He wrote a letter to his brother where he states, "Vassar seems to be very interested in communism. And a great deal of warm debating is going on among the students of Mary's class, which I think is an excellent thing. People of that age ought to be radical anyhow." It was during this period that she first met John F. Kennedy when she attended a dance at Choate Rosemary Hall.

After she graduated from Vassar, Meyer began working as a journalist for United Press. By this time she had joined the American Labor Party. Joining that party resulted in the Federal Bureau of Investigation opening a file on her political activities. Like her parents, Meyer was a pacifist. In 1944 she met Cord Meyer. Meyer was a marine who had suffered serious combat injuries that resulted in him losing an eye. At the time the two had similar political views and on April 19, 1945, they were married. Shortly after their marriage the couple attended the conference held in San Francisco that resulted in the establishment of the United Nations. Cord Meyer went as an aide to Harold Stassen while his wife covered the conference for the North American Newspaper Alliance.

During this time period the Meyer's started a family. Their first son Quentin was born in 1945, followed by Michael in 1947. The couple had a third son named mark who was born in 1950. With three small children, Meyer settled into the role of being a housewife.

Mary Pinchot Meyer was found shot and killed near her Georgetown home.

The couple at this time supported the idea of world government. However in 1950 after the family moved to Cambridge, Cord Meyer lost his enthusiasm for the idea. It was also around this time that he began working secretly for the Central Intelligence Agency (CIA). In 1951 he officially became an employee of the agency where he became a key player in "Operation Mockingbird" a covert operation designed to move the American media toward the positions supported by the CIA.

The Meyer family now moved to Washington D.C. and settled in Georgetown. The couple was very visible in Georgetown social circles that included people like Katherine Graham, Clark Clifford and the high ranking CIA official by the name of Richard M. Bissell. In 1953 Senator Joe McCarthy accused Cord Meyer of being a communist. Allen Dulles was successful in defending Meyer, and he was able to keep his position with the CIA. In the summer of 1954 John F. Kennedy and his wife Jackie purchased Hickory Hill a house close to that of the Meyers. Mary Meyer and Jackie Kennedy became good friends and often went on walks together. As the Meyer's political views grew apart, it put a strain on their relationship. In 1956 their son Michael was killed after being hit by a car close to the family home. In 1958 Mary Meyer filed for a divorce. In the filing she alleged "extreme cruelty, mental in nature, which seriously injured her health, destroyed her happiness, rendered further cohabitation unendurable and compelled the parties to separate."

After the divorce Meyer and her two surviving sons remained in the family home. She began painting in a garage at the home of her sister who was married to the *Washington Post's* Ben Bradlee. In her book *A Very Private Woman* Nina Burleigh, who knew Meyer personally, wrote that during this period Meyer "was out looking for fun and getting in trouble along the way."

During this period Meyer began running into John Kennedy at social functions and parties. Many were aware that he was very much attracted to her, but Meyer knew about his womanizing and for a time that put her off. In addition Kennedy's plans to make a run for the presidency were, by this time well known, and she thought his womanizing was reckless.

After Kennedy's election Meyer evidently changed her mind. Beginning in October 1961, she became a frequent visitor to the White House. The general consensus is that once their relationship became intimate Kennedy and Meyer got together at least 30 times. In addition it is generally believed that on her visits to the White House Meyer brought with her marijuana and in some cases LSD. Meyer during this period told some friends she was keeping a diary.

How close was the relationship between Kennedy and Meyer? In an interview with Nina Burleigh, Kennedy aide Myer Feldman responded to a question with the following, "I think he might have thought more of her than some of the other women and discussed things that were on his mind not just social gossip." Burleigh wrote that "Mary might actually have been a force for peace during some of the most frightening years of the cold war."

In 1976 Ron Rosenbaum and Phillip Nobile wrote an article titled, "The Curious Aftermath of JFK's Best and Brightest Affair." They refer to Mary in the article as the "secret lady Ottoline of Camelot." They claimed to have been granted an interview with a source who did not wish to be identified but was in a unique position to comment on the couple's relationship. The interview went as follows:

"How could a woman so admired for her integrity as Mary Meyer traduce her friendship with Jackie Kennedy?"

"They weren't friends" was the curt response.
"Did JFK actually love Mary Meyer?"
"I think so."
"Then why would he carry on an affair simultaneously with Judith Exner?'
"My friend there's a difference between sex and love."
"But why Mary Meyer over all other women?"
"He was an unusual man. He wanted the best."

In 1983 former Harvard professor Timothy Leary claimed that Meyer visited him and said that she was involved in a plan to avert nuclear war by convincing powerful men in Washington to take mind altering drugs with a goal of having them reach the conclusion that the Cold War was meaningless. According to Leary the purpose of her visit was to find out how to conduct LSD sessions with these men. When Leary suggested that Mary bring the men here so he could conduct the session she responded by saying that was impossible since the man she was involved with was much too powerful.

In her book Burleigh confirms Meyer's own use of LSD and her involvement with Leary which occurred at the same time she was involved with Kennedy. While Burleigh draws no conclusions as to whether Kennedy participated in any LSD sessions she does note that the timing of her visits to Leary coincided with Meyer's known meetings with Kennedy. During a 1990 interview Leary was asked point blank whether he had any doubt that Kennedy was using LSD in the White House with Meyer. He responded by saying, "I can't say that." He pointed out that it was his assumption that Meyer had proposed to take LSD with Kennedy but that he had no proof it had actually happened. Pressed, Leary agreed, that it was possible, even likely, that Kennedy had taken LSD, but he would go no further than that.

On September 24, 1963, Kennedy went with both Meyer and her sister Tony for a visit to the family's Grey Tower estate in Milford, Pennsylvania. The purpose of the President's visit was to dedicate a gift from the Pinchot family to the United States Forest Service. The gift included a large piece of land and the Pinchot mansion which had served as the home of Meyer's uncle and former Pennsylvania Governor Gifford Pinchot. As documented by Peter Janney in his excellent book *Mary's Mosaic* Tony had no idea about the affair between her sister and the President. She said, "I always felt he liked me as much as Mary. You could say there was a little rivalry." Ironically on the same day as the dedication, the United States Senate ratified Kennedy's Limited Nuclear Test Ban Treaty with the Soviet Union and the United Kingdom.

Two months later, after Kennedy was assassinated, Leary said he received a phone call from Meyer who sobbed and said "They couldn't control him anymore. He was changing too fast ... They've covered everything up. I gotta come see you. I'm afraid."

There is no way to document where Meyer was when she got word of the assassination. She spent the night at a friend's house in Georgetown. The friend recalled that Meyer was very sad and that they both cried but said very little.

As detailed in Janney's book Meyer spent the next year trying to solve the mystery surrounding Kennedy's death. From the first she was sure it had been a conspiracy, and one of the first people Meyer questioned was Kennedy aide Kenneth O'Donnell. O'Donnell respected Meyer largely because he was aware of the role she had played in the president's life. During one interview O'Donnell said he, "feared she had a hold on Jack." O'Donnell and another Kennedy aide by the name of Dave Powers were riding in the car directly behind Kennedy in the motorcade. Both were combat veterans of World

War II. O'Donnell told Meyers about what he and Powers had witnessed that day, the smell of gunpowder and the fact that at least two shots were fired from behind the fence on what has become known as the grassy knoll. Twenty-five years later his account was confirmed by Speaker of the House Tip O'Neill. O'Neill recalled a conversation he had at a dinner with O'Donnell and Powers five years after the assassination. The two told O'Neill that two shots had come from behind the fence. When O'Neill responded, "That's not what you told the Warren Commission." O'Donnell readily agreed saying that the FBI told him it couldn't have happened that way so he testified the way "they wanted me to" because I didn't want to cause more pain or trouble for the family.

Dave Powers was interviewed on the radio in 1991 where he basically told the same story. It was around the time that Oliver Stone's film JFK had been released. After the broadcast Woody Woodland, who had done the interview, was walking Powers to his car when he asked Powers if he had seen the film. He replied that he had. Woodland then asked, "What did you think of it?" Powers responded, "I think they got it right." "Really?" was the reply from a surprised Woodland. "Yes,' said Powers, "we were riding into an ambush. They were shooting from behind the fence." Woodland pointed out that was different from what Powers told the Warren Commission. Powers also admitted that that was true but added he had been told not to say that by the FBI.

Meyer began collecting information on the assassination. One of the people she sought out with regard to the assassination was William Walton, a gay man who had been her escort to many White House social affairs. Walton met Kennedy after World War II, and the two developed a close friendship. Kennedy's wife Jackie enjoyed Walton's company as well and when Kennedy was elected president, Walton enjoyed an almost unchecked access to the White House, and soon he became a close friend of Bobby Kennedy's as well. When Walton met Mary he found her to be distraught with grief. He told her that Bobby suspected something far deeper than Lee Harvey Oswald when it came to the death of his brother. He said Bobby had a plan to take back the presidency, but that it would be years before he could do anything about his brother's death. Despite this information Meyer continued her quest to learn more about Kennedy's death.

In the summer of 1964, Meyer began telling friends that she believed someone had been in her house while she was away. She told another friend that on one occasion she saw someone leaving the house as she was entering. Her friends confirmed that Meyer was frightened by these incidents. By this time Meyer had told a friend, Ann Truitt, that she had kept a diary that detailed her relationship with Kennedy. She asked Truitt to retrieve the diary should anything happen to her.

On October 12, 1964, Meyer was taking her daily walk on the Chesapeake and Ohio towpath in Georgetown. Henry Wiggins a car mechanic was working on a car on Canal Road when he heard a woman scream, "Someone help me, someone help me." Almost immediately he heard two gunshots. Wiggins ran to the edge of a wall overlooking the towpath where he saw a black man wearing a light jacket, dark pants and a dark cap standing over the body of a white woman. Wiggins would later tell police that the man was between 5 feet 8 inches to 5 feet 10 inches and weighed about 185 pounds. According to Wiggins the man turned and looked at him for a few seconds and after shoving something in his pocket turned and walked away disappearing down an embankment.

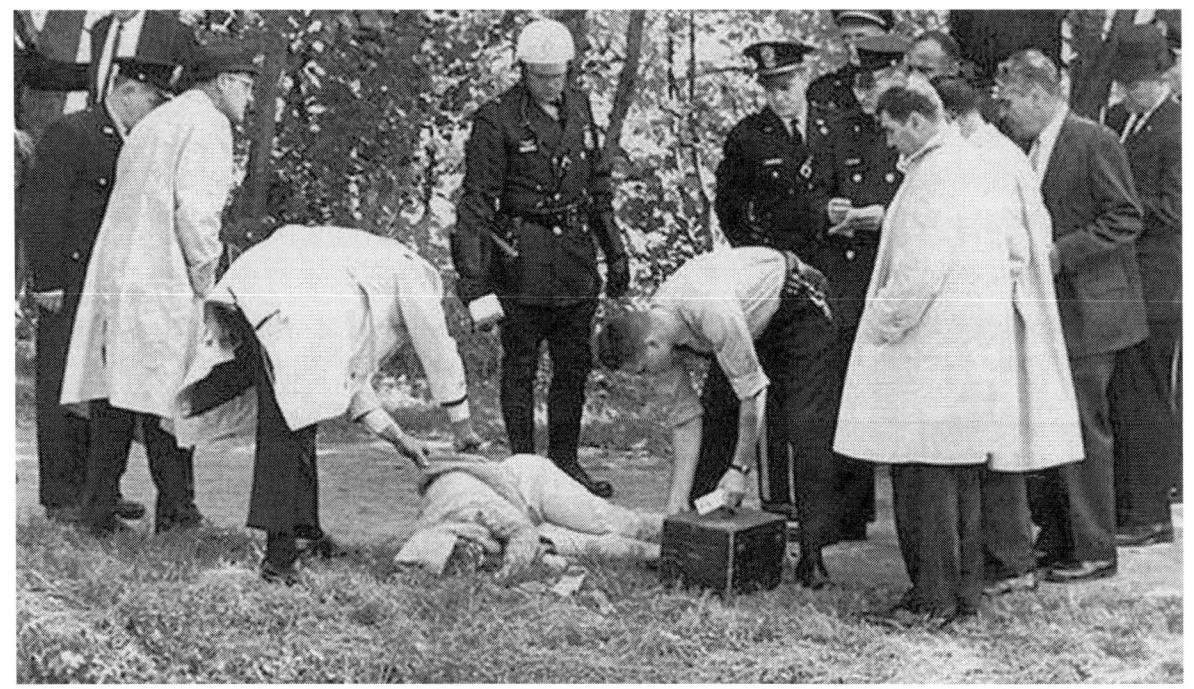

Mary Pinchot Meyer's murder scene

Meyer's body was taken to the Washington D. C. morgue where an autopsy was performed by Deputy Coroner Doctor Linwood L. Rayford, a man who, by this time, performed more than 400 such procedures on gunshot victims. He found that Meyer had been shot twice: once in the head and once in the back. He concluded that both shots were fired at close range. According to the doctor Meyer probably survived the first shot to the head though it would have rendered her unconscious. He noted that the second shot was fired with remarkable precision. That bullet severed the aorta and death would have been instantaneous. That bothered Rayford because he felt that it indicated that whoever killed Meyer was a professional.

Meanwhile the police had arrested a black man, Ray Crump, who was found in the area of the shooting and who stood 5 foot 4 inches tall. They conducted tests to show that he had fired the gun that killed Meyer but found no nitrates on either his hands or his clothes. They conducted an extensive search for two days that included the use of scuba divers and actually draining the canal near the scene of the murder. No gun could be found. Crump was eventually acquitted (for a detailed account of that story the authors strongly recommend Janney's book *Mary's Mosaic*).

Ann Truitt was in Tokyo when Meyer was killed. She called Meyer's brother-in-law Ben Bradlee and told him about the diary. The next day Bradlee and his wife went to the Meyer home when they arrived it was locked and when they entered they found James Angleton, The CIA counterintelligence chief already searching for the diary. There are various reports of what happened to it. Some believe Angleton burned it while others believe it remains in someone's possession.

In February of 2001, a writer asked Cord Meyer about Mary Meyer. He responded by saying it had been a bad time because his father had died that same year. Getting back to Mary Meyer the writer asked who could have committed such a heinous crime.

Cord Meyer responded, "The same sons of bitches that killed John F. Kennedy."

Mary Pinchot Meyer was laid to rest in the Pinchot family plot in the Milford, Pennsylvania cemetery. She lies next to her son Michael.

If You Go:

Meyer's uncle and former Governor of Pennsylvania **Gifford Pinchot** (see *Keystone Tombstones Volume 1*) is housed in a large mausoleum in the Milford Cemetery. Just across the road from his gravesite is the grave of **Charles Henry Van Wyck**. He was a New York Congressman, a Senator from Nebraska and a Brigadier general in the Civil War (See *Keystone Tombstones Civil War*, chapter 30)

On February 22, 1861, Van Wyck survived an assassination attempt in Washington. The attempt took place on the same night that an attempt was made to assassinate President-Elect Lincoln in Baltimore. The attack on Van Wyck was apparently motivated by a harsh anti-slavery speech he delivered on the floor of the house. In the speech he denounced the southern states for the "crime against the laws of God and nature." He fought off the attack and survived only because a book and papers that he carried in his breast pocket blocked the thrust of a Bowie knife.

Also buried in the Milford Cemetery is **General Daniel Brodhead**. He fought with George Washington on Long Island and wintered with the Continental Army at Valley Forge in 1777-1778.

This modest tombstone marks the final resting place of a woman who refused to believe the conclusions reached by the Warren Commission.

General Daniel Brodhead

Joe Paterno

18.
JoePa

Joe Paterno
County: Centre
Town: State College
Cemetery: Spring Creek Presbyterian Cemetery
Address: Country Club Rd.

It's probably hard to find an adult in Pennsylvania who hasn't heard of Joe Paterno. "JoePa," as he was commonly known, was the College Football Hall-of-Fame coach of the Pennsylvania State University Nittany Lions from 1966 until 2011.

Joseph Vincent Paterno was born in Brooklyn, New York on December 21, 1926. His parents, Florence and Angelo Paterno, stressed hard work and the importance of education. Angelo embodied this belief as he worked to support his family while attending law school. He got his law degree when he was 40 years old. Apparently the drive and determination rubbed off on Joe.

Joe attended St. Edmond's Grammar School and Brooklyn Prep High School, where he was a very good student. In the Flatbush section of Brooklyn, the Paterno family was known for its spirited arguments and debates over dinner which were encouraged by the parents.

As a senior at Brooklyn Prep, Joe and his younger brother, George (a junior), gained notoriety throughout the New York metropolitan area for their exploits on the football field (not to mention the basketball court). Asked years later to describe Joe's football abilities, a high school teammate of Paterno's stated, "He couldn't run, he couldn't kick, he couldn't pass." The teammate quickly added however, "All he could do was win." The Paterno-led Brooklyn Prep football team headed into its final game of the 1943 season undefeated, and considered by many to be one of the best teams on the American eastern seaboard. Their opponent in that final game? St. Cecilia's, a Roman Catholic high school in Englewood, New Jersey. The coach of St. Cecilia? A 30-year-old fellow Brooklynite named Vince Lombardi. To motivate his players before the game, Lombardi read letters that were sent to him by friends in Brooklyn, telling Lombardi how great Paterno was and how Brooklyn Prep was going to destroy St. Cecilia's that day. Tired of hearing about the kid from Brooklyn, the St. Cecilia players came out extra riled up. (As it turned out, the letters hadn't come from anyone in Brooklyn; Lombardi himself had written the letters.)

Paterno hurt his left (throwing) shoulder in the first half of the game, and was briefly replaced by his backup. At halftime, he got a shot of Novocain so he could play in the second half, continuing the game essentially one-armed. In the second half, Lombardi employed a four-man defensive line, something which Brooklyn Prep had never seen before let alone been trained to deal with. After the game, Paterno and his teammates were stunned they had lost. Lombardi's St. Cecilia's squad was recognized as the top football team in the nation that year, in large part based on their victory over Brooklyn Prep.

Paterno graduated from Brooklyn Prep in 1944 and was quickly drafted into the Army. He was still in training stateside when World War II ended. He was discharged in time to matriculate at the start the 1946 school year. He decided to attend Brown University, where he would play quarterback and cornerback. His tuition was paid by wealthy Brown alumnus Everett "Busy" Arnold, a publisher and owner of Quality Comics. Quality Comics was a comic book company that was very successful in the 1930's and 1940's.

Truth be told, Paterno was not an outstanding football player. He didn't have loads of "raw talent." He wasn't terribly "fast." He wasn't exceptionally "strong," mostly due to the fact that he didn't possess a great deal of "size." But Joe was extremely intelligent, and boy could he inspire his teammates. In 1949, he led the Brown Bears to an 8-1 record. He snagged 14 interceptions during his Brown career, a school record which he shares to this day. He also returned kicks and played two seasons of basketball for Brown, where in his freshman year he was coached by Weeb Ewbank (who went on to be a Hall-of-Fame football coach, winning NFL titles with Baltimore and the New York Jets).

After graduating from Brown in 1950, Paterno fully expected to enter Boston University Law School. But fate intervened. His Brown Coach, "Rip" Engle, had just accepted the job as head coach at Penn State. Having admired Paterno's cerebral play as his coach at Brown (Engle said in 1949 that having Paterno at quarterback was "like having another coach on the field"), Engle offered Paterno a job to join him as his assistant at the small agricultural school in the middle of Pennsylvania. Figuring he could postpone law school and save up some money, Paterno accepted Rip's offer.

He must have liked it, considering he stayed a Penn State football coach for the next 62 years, turning down a number of NFL opportunities! He was promoted to the top assistant spot in 1964 and when Engle announced his retirement in February 1966, Paterno was named his successor the next day.

In the meantime, Joe planted roots amidst the agricultural setting State College provided. He married Suzanne Pohland of Latrobe, Pennsylvania in 1962. Between 1963 and 1972, the couple had five children, all of whom would go on to attend Penn State.

Penn State went 5-5 in Paterno's first year, but in his second year they compiled an 8-2-1 record and a Gator Bowl appearance. In this third (1968) and fourth (1969) years, Penn State recorded undefeated seasons en route to a 31-game unbeaten streak. In 1968, they were ranked number 2 in the final national poll, and finished in that same spot again in 1969 after beating Missouri in the Orange Bowl. The 1969 experience was particularly upsetting to Paterno. Both Texas and Arkansas were undefeated and playing each other in early December. President Nixon declared that the winner of that game would be the national champion. Texas won and Nixon presented the mythical "national championship plaque" to the Longhorns. A few years later, while speaking at Penn State's Spring 1973 commencement, Paterno would ask "How could Nixon know so little about Watergate in 1973 and so much about football in 1969?"

That autumn the Nittany Lions continued their outstanding play, led by running back John Capellettti (who would become the first Penn State player to win the Heisman Trophy). As in 1968 and 1969, Penn State was once again undefeated and untied (11-0) heading into its bowl game: the January 1, 1974 Orange Bowl against LSU. Penn State won, and afterwards Paterno told reporters:

"I had my own poll, the Paterno Poll. And the vote was unanimous. Penn State is number 1. I took the vote a few minutes ago."

Unfortunately for Penn State and its fans, the polls did not agree with JoePa. Penn State was ranked 5th in the final poll, behind #1 Notre Dame (11-0), #2 Ohio State (10-0-1), #3 Oklahoma (10-0-1), and #4 Alabama (11-1). Paterno paid to have championship rings made for every player on the team.

Ironically, when Penn State *was* voted as number one at the end of the 1982 season, they were *not* undefeated. They had lost a mid-season game to Alabama, but won seven straight games after that, including a win over Georgia in the Sugar Bowl.

Another shot at finishing the season ranked No. 1 came in 1986 after an 11-0 season. The only thing standing between #2-ranked Penn State and another championship? A Fiesta Bowl showdown with the undefeated, #1-ranked Miami Hurricanes.

The Jimmy Johnson-led Hurricanes had a firm grasp on the #1 ranking for most of that season. The team's star quarterback was Vinny Testaverde, the 1986 Heisman Trophy winner. Miami also featured All-Americans Jerome Brown and Bennie Blades on defense, future NFL Hall-of-Famer Michael Irvin at wide receiver, and running back Alonzo Highsmith. The Penn State defense harassed Testaverde into five interceptions and the underdog Nittany Lions won 14-10. Years later, Johnson would describe that year's Miami team as the most talented he had ever coached, and said that losing the Fiesta Bowl to Penn State remains the one loss in his entire career that still haunts him.

By this time, JoePa had become well-known for doing things his way. He expected his athletes to get an education. The graduation rate of his players was consistently above the national average. He refused to modernize the team's uniforms, refused to put players' names on the back of their jerseys, and was known for his gameday image - thick glasses, rolled up pants, white socks and Brooklyn accent.

He was also renowned for his charitable contributions to academics at Penn State. The Paternos have given the university over $4 million towards various departments and scholarships. After they helped raise $13.5 million for the 1997 expansion of the library, it was named after them. Paterno often joked that Penn State was the only campus that had a library named after a football coach and a sports arena (the Bryce Jordan Center) named after a former university president.

After earning the number one ranking at the end of the 1982 season, Paterno attended a meeting of the Board of Trustees where he urged them to raise entrance requirements and spend more money on the library. According to a story in *Sports Illustrated*, "it may go down as the only time in history that a coach yearned for a school the football team could be proud of." He called this meeting of athletics and academics a "Grand Experiment." Sue Paterno played a role too, often tutoring players at the team's study hall or even sometimes at their home.

Penn State had five undefeated, untied seasons under Paterno, winning a major bowl at the end of each of those seasons. Four of those teams (1968, 1969, 1973 and 1994) were not awarded a national championship - the lone exception being 1986.

Heading into the 1994 for what would turn out to be Penn State's final undefeated season under Paterno, Penn State had joined the Big Ten Conference. Its 38-20 victory over #12 Oregon in the Rose Bowl on January 2, 1995 capped a perfect 12-0 season.

Yet once again, the polls denied them the number one spot. Penn State finished second, behind Tom Osbourne's 13-0 Nebraska team, led by quarterback Tommy Frazier. The previous season had seen the Cornhuskers fall just short of their first national title under Osborne with a controversial Orange Bowl loss to Florida State 18–16. The 1994 offseason was dubbed "Unfinished Business" by the Huskers, in their quest to secure a national championship for the coming season.

The AP poll heading in to their respective October 29, 1994 games had Penn State ranked #1 and Nebraska #3. That day both teams won at home: Penn State defeated #21 Ohio State 63-14 at Beaver Stadium, while Nebraska beat visiting #2 Colorado 24-7. In the ensuing AP poll, not only did Nebraska supplant Colorado as expected, but it also leapfrogged over Penn State to claim the #1 spot (Penn State "slipped" to #2). The two teams would remain locked in those positions the rest of the way, each winning out the remainder of their respective regular season schedules and bowl games (Nebraska defeated #3 Miami in the Orange Bowl 24-17 on January 1, 1995).

Under JoePa's reign, Penn State made a record 37 bowl appearances and won a record 24 times. He is the only coach to win the Rose, Orange, Fiesta, Sugar and Cotton Bowl games at least once. His teams finished in the top 10 in national rankings 29 times. In 2001, Penn State honored Paterno with a statue outside Beaver Stadium - a stadium that underwent six capacity expansions during his tenure, increasing from 46,284 seats in 1966 to 106,572 in 2001. He was named the American Football Coaches' Association Coach of the Year Award five times (1968, 1978, 1982, 1986 and 2005) and received dozens of other coaching and sportsman awards. In May 2006, Paterno was elected to the College Football Hall of Fame. He even had an award named after him in 2010: the Maxwell Football Club of Philadelphia established the Joseph V. Paterno Award, to be awarded annually to the coach who has made a positive impact on his university, his players and his community.

At the time of his death in 2012, Paterno had accumulated 409 wins, the most ever by a major college coach. Paterno offered up many pearls of wisdom during that legendary 1973 commencement speech, including this statement, which has since been often repeated: "Success without honor is an unseasoned dish; it will satisfy your hunger, but it won't taste good."

If only the story ended here!

On November 5, 2011, a former Penn State defensive coordinator, Jerry Sandusky, was arrested and charged with 52 counts of sexual abuse of young boys over a 15-year period. Sandusky had served as an assistant coach under Joe Paterno for almost 30 years. In 1977, Sandusky founded The Second Mile, a non-profit charity serving Pennsylvania's underprivileged and at-risk youth. Now Sandusky was accused of meeting his victims through The Second Mile, and many of the incidents were alleged to have taken place in Penn State facilities, including the Penn State football locker room.

A grand jury investigation reported that then-graduate assistant Mike McQueary had told Paterno in 2002 that he witnessed Sandusky abusing a 10-year-old boy in the football team's shower facilities. Paterno reported it to his boss, the Athletic Director, and did nothing more. Reports indicate that no one ever contacted the police.

The news rocked the sports world and beyond. While prosecutors did not accuse Paterno of any wrongdoing, he was criticized for his failure to follow up on McQueary's report. Sandusky continued to have unrestricted and unsupervised access to the

Paterno statue before it was removed (courtesy of Bob And Holly Frymoyer)

University's facilities and affiliation with the football program until his arrest on November 5, 2011.

On November 9, as a result of the growing outrage and swirling controversy, Paterno announced he would retire at the end of the season. Later that evening however, the Penn State Board of Trustees decided to reject Paterno's offer to resign, instead voting to relieve him of coaching duties effective immediately. The Board notified him of their decision over the phone. At the same meeting, the University President resigned rather than face being fired.

Paterno's dismissal was met with violence from students and alumni. That night several thousand Penn State students chanting Paterno's name rioted in the streets, hurling rocks, tearing down street signs and overturning a news van.

On November 18, Paterno's family announced that he was suffering from lung cancer. He was hospitalized on January 13, 2012, and nine days later died on January 22, 2012. Paterno's funeral was held in State College on January 25. About 750 mourners attended a private ceremony, after which thousands lined the route of the funeral procession. On January 26, a public memorial service was held at the Bryce Jordan Center and an estimated 12,000 people attended. JoePa is buried in a modest grave in Spring Creek Presbyterian Cemetery in State College, just a few short miles away from Beaver Stadium.

The scandal had far-reaching effects on the University and on Joe Paterno's legacy. On June 22, 2012, Sandusky was found guilty on all but three of the counts against him. On October 9, 2012 he was sentenced to a minimum of 30 years and maximum of 60 years in prison. Judge John Cleland stated that he intentionally avoided a sentence with a large number of years, saying it would be "too abstract" and also said to Sandusky that the sentence he handed down had the "unmistakable impact of saying 'the rest of your life.'"

In July 2013, a report on an investigation commissioned by Penn State Board of Trustees and conducted by former FBI director Louis Freeh was released. The report stated that Paterno, as well as the University's president, vice-president and athletic director, had known about allegations of child abuse on Sandusky's part as early as 1998, and were complicit in failing to disclose them. The report concluded that the four men had "concealed Sandusky's activities from the Board of Trustees, the University community and authorities." The report criticized Paterno for his failure to "alert the entire football staff in order to prevent Sandusky from bringing another child into the Lasch Building" [the football team's 89,000 square-foot indoor facility on the Penn State campus, just a short walk from Beaver Stadium].

A mere 11 days after the Freeh report, the NCAA announced sanctions against Penn State. The sanctions included a post-season ban, a large fine, the loss of scholarships and the vacating of all wins from 1998 to 2011. This amounted to 111 wins, including 6 bowl victories, and stripped Penn State of their shared Big Ten titles in 2005 and 2008. It also removed the 111 wins from Paterno's record, dropping him from first to 12th on the NCAA's all-time wins list (two wins behind legendary University of Delaware coach, Tubby Raymond). Penn State accepted the sanctions.

In the weeks that followed, Nike Inc. removed Paterno's name from the Joe Paterno Child Development Center at the company's headquarters in Beaverton, Oregon. Brown University, Paterno's alma mater, announced it would remove Paterno's name from its annual award honoring outstanding male freshman athletes. The NCAA

Final resting place of the legendary coach who obviously has not been forgotten.

revoked Paterno's 2011 Gerald R. Ford leadership award. The lifesize statue of Paterno outside Beaver Stadium was removed by the university.

The story continues to develop and will for some time to come. There are many arguments and disagreements about Paterno's role. Penn State's former president, vice-president and athletic director were all indicted and are awaiting trial at the time of this publication. There have been civil lawsuits and settlements, and there may be more. Additional investigations are ongoing, and there may be more. Books have been written, and there will be more. We may never know the full story. There has been much pain and much conflict over Paterno's role, his culpability, his treatment by Penn State, the grand jury investigation, the Freeh report, The Second Mile, and the NCAA's response. Of particular interest at the time of this writing is an ongoing lawsuit filed by the Paterno family (along with several members of the Penn State Board of Trustees, and a number of faculty, former players and coaches) against the NCAA. They assert that the Freeh report—which the NCAA relied for its actions—is fundamentally wrong, incomplete and inaccurate. They further allege that the consent decree with Penn State which set forth the various sanctions was hastily imposed on the University, completely disregarding the rights of the affected parties.

Just before his death, Paterno told the *Washington Post*, "I didn't know exactly how to handle it, so I backed away." Then he added, "I'm sick about it."

So too are a whole lot of others.

Governor Beaver

If You Go:

Union Cemetery in nearby Bellefonte has many interesting graves, including:

Pennsylvania's governor during the Civil War, **Andrew Curtin**, (*see Keystone Tombstones: Civil War*, Chapter 29);

James Adams Beaver, who was a Civil War general, later elected governor of Pennsylvania (1887-1891) and after whom Penn State's Beaver Stadium is named; and

Penn State's first president, **Evan Pugh.**, who served in the University's highest post from 1859 until his death from typhoid in 1864 at the age of 36. An agricultural chemist, he was responsible for securing Penn State's designation in 1863 as a land-grant institution under the Morrill Land Grant Act. Today, the highest honor the University can bestow on a faculty member is the title "Evan Pugh Professor."

If you are looking for a great place to stop for refreshments, the area is full of wonderful eating and drinking establishments. The possibilities boggled our minds.

19.
Life Is a Song Worth Singing

Teddy Pendergrass
County: Montgomery
Town: Bala Cynwyd
Cemetery: West Laurel Hill
Address: 215 Belmont Avenue

Theodore DeReese Pendergrass was a major figure in the American soul and rhythm and blues genres as both a signer and a songwriter during the 1970's and 80's. He first rose to fame as the lead singer of the group "Harold Melvin and the Blue Notes" in the 70's before having a successful solo career. Even after he was severely injured in an auto accident, he fought through arduous physical rehabilitation to be able to continue to sing and continue his magnificent career.

Teddy Pendergrass was born in Philadelphia's Thomas Jefferson Hospital on March 26, 1950. His parents Ida and Jesse Pendergrass were both children of South Carolina sharecroppers. Ida's multiple miscarriages before Teddy was born prompted her to name him Theodore, which means "God's Gift."

Jesse Pendergrass left the family when Teddy was a small child and according to newspaper accounts, Teddy did not see his biological father again until 1961, one year before Jesse was murdered by a neighborhood friend over a gambling debt.

Teddy's early years were filled with love and affection from his mother and several aunts. He grew up in Philadelphia and sang often at church. When he was 10 years old, he was ordained as a youth minister. His singing in the McIntyre Elementary School choir and The All-City Stetson Junior High School choir was where he discovered his ability and discovered his taste for singing in front of large audiences.

He attended Thomas Edison High School, and when he was 15 years old his mother gave him a set of drums, which he taught himself how to play. He dropped out of high school in 11th grade to pursue a career as a musician. He worked with a number of R&B and doo-wop groups and in 1968 took a job as the drummer for a group called "The Cadillacs." The Cadillacs, along with Harold Melvin and the Blue Notes, were the best known R&B bands in Philadelphia. In 1970, the two groups merged and several of the Cadillacs (including Pendergrass) joined the Blue Notes. Soon after, Harold Melvin asked Teddy to become the lead singer and from there the Blue Notes took off.

They landed a recording deal with Philadelphia International Records, and their first single - "I Miss You" - became an instant hit on the Pop and R&B charts. The song was written for the Dells, but they passed on it. The group's follow-up single was intended for fellow Philadelphian Patti LaBelle, but her group "LaBelle" could not get their schedule together, and it went to Harold Melvin and the Blue Notes. The song - "If You Don't Know Me By Now" - brought the group to the mainstream. It reached No. 3 on the Pop charts and No. 1 on the Soul chart.

A series of hits followed, such as: "Wake Up Everybody;" "Bad Luck;" "To Be True;"

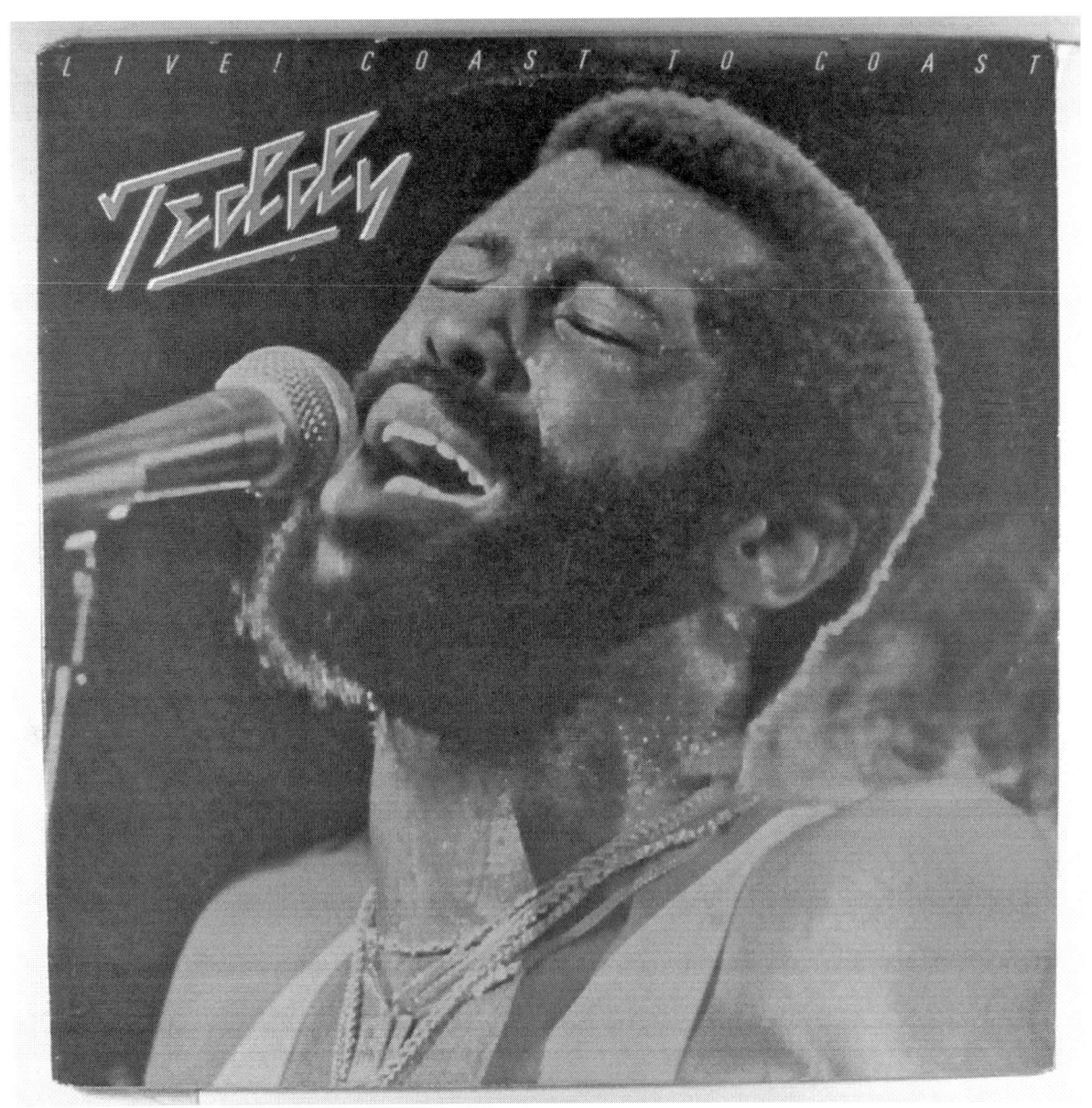

Teddy Pendergrass album cover

and "The Love I Lost." Meanwhile, however, trouble was developing behind the scenes between Pendergrass and Melvin. In 1976, they parted company. For a while, there were two groups called the Blue Notes, one led by Pendergrass and the other by Melvin.

The confusion ended in 1977 when Pendergrass officially went solo with the release of his first album, "Teddy Pendergrass." It sold more than a million copies and generated several No. 1 hits. The concerts that supported the album were a smash and showed him as a powerful force as a solo artist. More success followed. Between 1977 and 1981, Pendergrass had five consecutive platinum albums and a number of national awards such as the Billboard New Artist Award (1977), two Grammy nominations, and an American Music Award.

This beautiful monument marks the final resting place of the great soul and blues singer Teddy Pendergrass (plus a bonus reflection of Joe Farrell).

Pendergrass' manager noticed at his sold-out solo performances that a huge portion of his audiences were women. That led to a series of "women-only" concerts. At some of these concerts, audience members were given chocolate teddy bear-shaped lollipops to lick. Around that time, comedian Eddie Murphy made several humorous observations about Pendergrass in his landmark HBO special "Delirious." He began by describing Pendergrass as a "dude with a masculine voice," whose singing style and lyrics such as "You got, you got, YOU GOT WHAT I NEED!!" would lead to women throwing their panties on stage.

By early 1982, Pendergrass was the leading R&B male artist of his day. But on March 18th of that year, Pendergrass was involved in an auto accident in Philadelphia.

He lost control of his car, hit a guardrail, crossed the opposite traffic lane and hit two trees. He and his passenger, a friend, Tenika Watson, were trapped in the wreckage for 45 minutes. Watson was unhurt, but Pendergrass suffered a spinal cord injury, leaving him paralyzed from the chest down.

In 1984, he decided to restart his career from a wheelchair after arduous physical and psychotherapy as well as several surgeries. His contract with Philadelphia International had run out, and he struggled to find a recording deal. He got a deal with Asylum Records and released his ninth studio album "Love Language," which included a pop ballad called "Hold Me" featuring a then-unknown Whitney Houston. The album did well, peaking at No. 38 on Billboard.

In July 1985, Teddy Pendergrass made an emotional return to the concert stage for the first time since the accident at the historic Live Aid concert in Philadelphia. In front of a live audience of 100,000 and an estimated viewing audience of 1.5 billion people, Pendergrass tearfully thanked fans for all the well-wishes, support and prayers, and performed the song "Reach Out and Touch."

In 1987, Pendergrass married Karen Smith, his longtime girlfriend. They divorced in 2003. In 1988, his album entitled "Joy" brought him a Grammy nomination and two hit singles. He continued to record and release albums throughout the 80's and 90's but never regained the prestige and success he once enjoyed.

In 1998, Pendergrass published his autobiography, *Truly Blessed*, which got a good review from *The New York Times*' Eric Nash, who wrote: "The book is both a richly textured history of Pendergrass' musical roots in the creative explosion of 70's soul that shaped his gruff, sexy style, and an unflinching look at what it is like to be disabled."

In 2006, Pendergrass announced his retirement from the music business and met Joan Williams whom he married in 2008. The following year, he did appear and sing at a concert in his honor, held at the Kimmel Center in Philadelphia. The show was called "Teddy 25: A Celebration of Life, Hope and Possibilities." It marked the 25th anniversary of his accident and was a star-studded fundraiser for the Teddy Pendergrass Alliance, a non-profit organization which has raised awareness of quality-of-life issues for people with spinal cord injuries.

Pendergrass was diagnosed with colon cancer in 2009 and died of complications after surgery on January 13, 2010, in Bryn Mawr Hospital in suburban Philadelphia. He is buried in a beautiful grave in West Laurel Hill Cemetery in Bala Cynwyd, Montgomery County.

If You Go:

West Laurel Hill Cemetery is a large, beautiful cemetery containing many graves of interesting and historical people, two of whom are featured in chapters in this Volume:

Television broadcast journalist and "The Today Show" host **Dave Garroway** (1913-1982) - *see* Chapter 11; and

Brilliant saxophonist **Grover Washington, Jr.** (1943-1999) - *see* Chapter 28.

Two famous psychologists are also buried in West Laurel Hill:

Almost any Introduction to Psychology book will contain a reference to the work of **Frederick Winslow Taylor** (1856-1915), who is regarded as the father of scientific management; and

Helen Bradford Thompson Woolley (1874-1947), who was a leading force in establishing child development studies in the United States.

Two famous sculptors (father and son) are also buried in West Laurel Hill:

Alexander Milne Calder (1846-1923), who is best known for the architectural sculpture of Philadelphia City Hall; and

Alexander's son, **A. Stirling Calder** (1870-1945), who is best known for the sculpture referred to as *George Washington as President, Accompanied by Wisdom and Justice* (which appears on the Washington Square Arch in New York City), and also for the Swann Memorial Fountain sculpture in Philadelphia, which is in the center of Logan Circle.

Other notable graves are those of:

Anna Jarvis (1864-1948), the founder of the Mother's Day holiday;

Hyman Aaron "Hy" Lit (1934-2007), the famous disc jockey and pioneer of rock-and-roll radio; and

Henry Williams (1834-1917), a rare, peacetime Medal of Honor recipient, who was given the award for his valiant repair work during a storm that saved the *USS Constitution* in 1879.

Frederick Winslow Taylor

Dramatic representation of Molly Pitcher

20.
From Molly Pitcher to Black Hawk Down

Molly Pitcher (Mary Ludwig)
County: Cumberland
Town: Carlisle
Cemetery: Old Public Graveyard (or "Old Graveyard")
Address: South Bedford & East South Streets

Molly Pitcher was a nickname given to a woman who fought in the Battle of Monmouth, during the American Revolutionary War. Her real name was Mary Ludwig. There is disagreement among scholars about several important details of her life, beginning with her date of birth. Her cemetery marker indicates that she was born on October 13, 1744, but others point to evidence suggesting it may have actually been October 13, 17**5**4. Her father is believed to have been a butcher, but he may have been a dairy farmer. There is little doubt that Mary was raised a hard worker. In 1768, she was sent to Carlisle, Pennsylvania, to become a servant in the home of Dr. William Irvine. The following year she married a local barber named William Hays.

Five years later, on July 12, 1774, in a meeting in the Presbyterian Church in Carlisle, Mary's employer (Dr. Irvine) organized a town boycott of British goods as a protest of the Tea Act of 1773. Mary's husband's name (William Hays) appears on a list of people who were charged with enforcing the boycott. In 1775, when the Revolutionary War began, William Hays enlisted in the Colonial Army.

After her husband's enlistment, Mary at first stayed in Carlisle and then went to live with her parents near Philadelphia (so that she could be closer to her husband's regiment). During the winter of 1777, Mary joined her husband at the Continental Army's winter camp at Valley Forge. She joined a group of "camp followers," who were led by Martha Washington. These women were of great importance to the army. As a general rule, women were not allowed to fight as soldiers. Instead, they cooked and washed the soldiers' clothes. They gathered and preserved food and supplies, and they repaired uniforms, blankets and other items. They cared for the sick, wounded and dying soldiers.

In the spring of 1778, the Continental Army was retrained under Baron von Steuben. During this time, William Hays trained as an artilleryman. Mary Hays and other camp followers served as "water girls" during the training, carrying water to drilling infantry troops. Artillerymen also needed a constant supply of water to cool down the hot cannon barrels and to soak the rag ("rammer rag") tied to the end of the ramrod with which they cleaned sparks and gunpowder out of the barrel after each shot.

The term "Molly Pitcher" was commonly used by Continental Army soldiers. It resulted from a combination of the name "Molly" (a widely-used nickname at the time for women named Mary or Margaret) and the term "pitcher" (the containers of water women carried on the battlefield).

The Battle of Monmouth took place on June 28, 1778, in modern-day Freehold, New Jersey. The Continental Army under General George Washington attacked the rear of the British Army column commanded by Lieutenant General Sir Henry Clinton as they left Monmouth Court House. With a high of over 100 degrees Fahrenheit that day, both sides lost almost as many men to heat stroke as to the enemy. It was during that battle that Mary Ludwig Hays earned the nickname "Molly Pitcher," becoming one of the most popular female images of the Revolutionary War.

Just before the battle started, Mary found a spring to serve as her water supply (there are currently two different places within Monmouth Battlefield State Park that are marked as the "Molly Pitcher Spring"). She spent the early part of the day carrying water under heavy fire from British troops. Sometime during the battle, Mary saw her husband collapse either from heat exhaustion or because he was wounded (but regardless managed to survive). For the rest of the day, Mary stepped in and continued to "swab and load" the cannon using her husband's ramrod. She continued to do this until the battle was over and according to accounts at one point - while loading a cartridge and having her feet far apart - a British musket ball flew between her legs and took off the lower part of her petticoat. Mary supposedly said, "Well that could have been worse" and went back to swabbing and loading. Later that evening the fighting stopped, and the British forces retreated and moved on. The Battle of Monmouth was seen as a major victory for Americans.

Mary's legendary heroism was noted, and she was commissioned as a sergeant by General Greene (or by some accounts by George Washington himself). From that day forward, she was known as "Sergeant Molly." An old Revolutionary rhyme tells the story:

Moll Pitcher she stood by her gun
And rammed the charges home, sir;
And thus on Monmouth bloody field
A sergeant did become, sir.

Until the close of the Revolutionary War, Molly Pitcher remained with the army and proved to be a beloved and valuable helping hand. After the war, she and her husband returned to Carlisle, and Mary went back to work as a domestic servant. In 1780, they had a son, John L. Hays. In 1786, William Hays died, and Mary married John McCauley, another veteran of the Revolutionary War. McCauley was a stone cutter. The marriage was reportedly not a happy one, and sometime between 1807 and 1810 John McCauley disappeared, and it is not known what became of him.

Mary Ludwig Hays McCauley was known throughout Carlisle as Molly Pitcher. She lived in a house on the corner of North and Bedford Streets, which has since been demolished. In 1822, the state legislature awarded Molly Pitcher a sum of $40 and subsequent annual payments of $40 each "for the rest of her life."

On January 22, 1852, Mary died in Carlisle and was buried in the old Carlisle Cemetery with military honors. Her grave was unmarked, and her obituary did not mention her war contributions.

In 1856, Mary's son John L. Hays died. His obituary noted that he "was a son of the ever-to-be-remembered heroine, the celebrated 'Molly Pitcher' whose deeds of daring are recorded in the annals of the Revolution and over whose remains a monument ought to be erected."

Molly Pitcher taking charge!

On July 4, 1876, the 100th anniversary of the Declaration of Independence, the citizens of Carlisle erected a white marble monument over Mary's grave. It commemorates "Molly Pitcher, the heroine of Monmouth."

To complicate the story, there is another similar heroic story of a woman in the Revolutionary War. Margaret Corbin was the wife of John Corbin of Philadelphia, who was also an artilleryman in the Continental Army. On November 12, 1776, John Corbin was killed defending Fort Washington in northern Manhattan. Margaret took his place at his cannon and continued to fire it until she was wounded. In 1779, she was awarded an annual pension by the Continental Congress. She was the first woman in the United States to receive a military pension. She is buried at West Point. Her nickname was "Captain Molly."

And so the name "Molly Pitcher" comes down to us as a symbol of courage and resourcefulness under fire. The story of Molly Pitcher was told for many generations. It inspired women of her time and captured the hearts of America. In 1928, Molly Pitcher was honored with an overprint on a U.S. postage stamp reading "MOLLY PITCHER" in capital letters. In 1978, the 200th anniversary of the Battle of Monmouth, Molly was pictured on an imprinted stamp on a postal card. She was further honored in World War II with the naming of the Liberty Ship *SS Molly Pitcher*, which was

Monument erected near her grave to honor her actions during the American Revolution.

launched and subsequently torpedoed on its maiden voyage on March 17, 1943, by a German U-Boat about 500 miles west of Lisbon, Spain.

The stretch of U.S. Route 11 between Shippensburg and the Pennsylvania-Maryland state line is known as the "Molly Pitcher Highway." There is a Molly Pitcher Ale House on 2nd Avenue and 85th Street in Manhattan, a Molly Pitcher Brewing Company in Atascadero, California, and a Molly Pitcher Inn in Red Bank, New Jersey, not far from the site of the Battle of Monmouth.

If You Go:
The **Old Public Graveyard** in Carlisle is the final resting place for 750 veterans from the Revolutionary War to Korea, including 550 Civil War veterans. Those buried there of particular interest include:

William Thompson, who served as a brigadier general in the Revolutionary War and was the first officer to be commissioned as a colonel in the United States Army;

Actual grave site of the American heroine.

John Montgomery, who was a founder of Dickinson College and saw action in the Revolution as a colonel and Commander of the Cumberland County Regiment and later served as a member of the Continental Congress; and

John Armstrong, a good friend of George Washington, who served in the Revolutionary War as a brigadier general and in the Continental Congress (and in whose honor Armstrong County, Pennsylvania was named).

Just 2.5 miles to the west of Old Graveyard is **Westminster Memorial Gardens** (1159 Newville Road), the final resting place for two American heroes:

John W. Minick, who was a staff sergeant in the United States Army when he was killed in action near Hurtgen, Germany, on November 21, 1944. On that day, he voluntarily led a small group of men through a minefield, single-handedly silenced two enemy machine gun emplacements, and engaged a company of German soldiers before he was killed while crossing a second minefield. For his actions he was awarded the Medal of Honor. His citation reads that he killed 22 enemy soldiers and captured 23 more. He was 36 years old.

Randall D. Shughart, who was a Special Forces soldier from Newville, Pennsylvania, and one of two soldiers (the other being Gary Gordon) who died trying to save the life of pilot Michael Durant, the only surviving member of a downed helicopter crew in Somalia on October 3, 1993. Shughart's actions - while costing him his own life - saved Durant's. For those actions, Shughart was awarded the Medal of Honor by President Clinton - the first soldier to be posthumously awarded the Medal of Honor since the Vietnam War. This incident was featured in the book and blockbuster Hollywood film "Black Hawk Down." The movie won two Oscars and was nominated for two more.

Shughart has been memorialized in many ways. A United States Navy ship, a training facility in Fort Polk, Louisiana, and his hometown post office in Newville all bear his name. Twenty years after his death, his modest grave was enhanced with a monument in his memory.

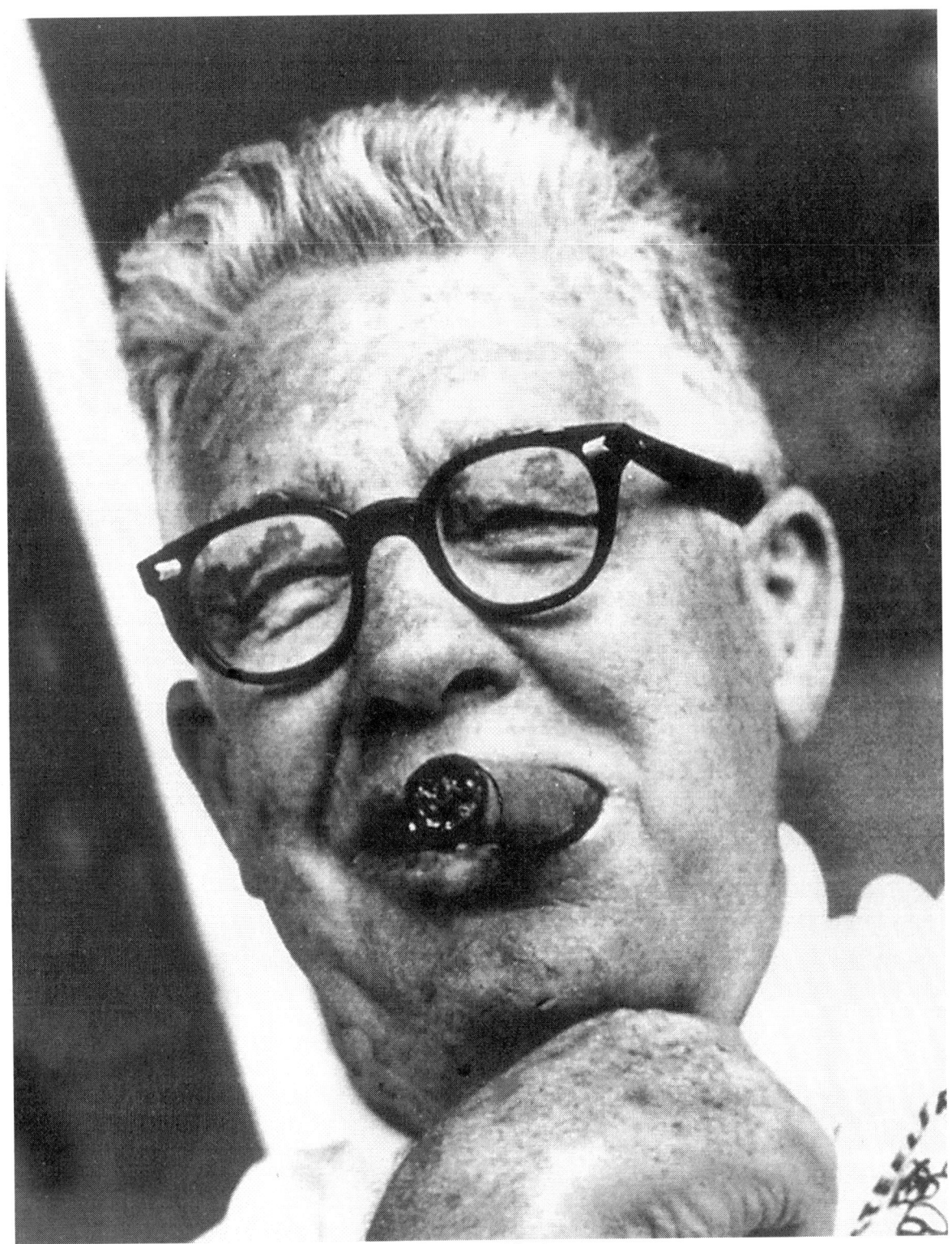

Art Rooney with cigar

21.
The Chief

Art Rooney
County: Allegheny
Town: Pittsburgh
Cemetery: Christ Our Redeemer
Address: 204 Cemetery Lane

Arthur Joseph "Art" Rooney, often referred to as "The Chief," was a man who has come to represent the triumph of the underdog. He was the founding owner of the Pittsburgh Steelers and is a member of the Pro Football Hall of Fame. The Steelers were once known as the "lovable losers" after managing only 24 victories in their first eight years. Today, the Steelers have won more Super Bowls than any other team in the history of the National Football League.

Rooney was born on January 27, 1901, in the small mining town of Coulter, near Pittsburgh. His great-grandparents were Irish immigrants who came to Canada during the potato famine of the 1840's. His parents, Dan and Maggie, settled on Pittsburgh's North Side in 1913, where they bought a three-story building in which Dan opened a saloon and the family lived above on the second floor. Three Rivers Stadium would later be built on this very site.

Rooney attended St. Peter's Parochial School and Duquesne University Prep School. He then attended Indiana Normal School (now Indiana University of Pennsylvania), Georgetown and Duquesne. He was always an exceptional athlete. When he was done with school he dedicated himself to sports. He won the AAU welterweight boxing title in 1918, and was named to the U.S. Olympic boxing team in 1920 but did not participate. Years later, he became a close fan and friend of the boxer, who was light heavyweight champion at the time, the Pittsburgh Kid, Billy Conn (see *Keystone Tombstones Volume 2*). As a matter of fact, it was Rooney who broke up the infamous fight between Billy Conn and his father-in-law that led to the cancellation of Conn's rematch with Joe Louis.

He played minor league baseball for the Flint (Michigan) Vehicles and Wheeling (West Virginia) Stogies. In 1925, he was the Wheeling player-manager and led the league in hits, runs, stolen bases and finished second in batting average.

He was twice offered football scholarships to Notre Dame by Knute Rockne but did not accept, and in the mid-1920's was offered baseball contracts with the Chicago Cubs and Boston Red Sox. He developed arm trouble while playing for Wheeling and that ended his major-league hopes.

Rooney's professional football career began with his founding an independent semi-professional football team based in Pittsburgh for which he coached and played. The team was originally called the "Hope-Harvey." The name was based on two things: (1) the firehouse where the team would dress and shower (which was located in the city's Hope ward); and (2) Dr. Walter Harvey, a physician who tended to the injured players.

Dr. Harvey never charged for his services to the team and the uniforms were homemade by the players or their family members. After a few years, a sponsor (Loeffler's Electronic Store) renamed the team after one of its best-selling products: the "Majestic Radios."

The team played for seven years as the Majestic Radios, but prior to the 1931 season the affiliation with Loeffler's ended and the team became known as the J.P. Rooneys to promote Art's brother James P. Rooney, who was running for election to the Pennsylvania House of Representatives (a race which James easily won). Art's semi-professional teams won two Western Pennsylvania Senior Independent Football Conference titles and he began to think about adding a Pittsburgh team to the National Football League (NFL).

The NFL began operating in 1920 and wanted a team in Pittsburgh due to the city's history with football and the popularity of the University of Pittsburgh football team. Pennsylvania's "blue laws" were however a major barrier. The blue laws prohibited sporting events on Sundays, when most of the NFL's games took place. When Pennsylvania relaxed its blue laws in 1933, Rooney saw an opportunity. On July 8 of that year, he bought an NFL franchise for $2,500 and named it the Pittsburgh Pirates. They were a member of the Eastern Division in a 10-team league which included the Chicago Bears, Green Bay Packers and New York Giants.

It has been said many times that Rooney bought the franchise with his winnings from betting on the horses, but that is uncertain. He did however win big at the Saratoga Course in 1936, where he won an amount he never revealed but various reports place it between $160,000 and $358,000 Depression-era dollars (or in today's money between about $2.7- $6.0 million dollars). It was no fluke, as Rooney is said to have been one of the greatest handicappers in the sport. He always remained interested in racing, and attended the Kentucky Derby and Irish Derby regularly. He acquired Yonkers Raceway in 1972, was an owner of Liberty Bell Racetrack near Philadelphia, and owned and operated Shamrock Farm in Maryland where he bred and trained thoroughbreds.

In 1935, Rooney used some of his winnings to hire a coach for his new football team: Joe Bach. Bach, who was one of Notre Dame's famed "seven mules" on the 1924 national championship team, coached the Pirates in the 1935 and 1936 seasons.

In 1938, Rooney sent shockwaves through the NFL by signing Byron "Whizzer" White to a record-breaking $15,000 contract. White was a college football star at Colorado, where he acquired the nickname "Whizzer." He postponed attending Oxford University on a Rhodes Scholarship for one year to play for the Pirates. He led the league in rushing and then departed for England. After Oxford, White played two years for the Detroit Lions, joined the Navy, fought in World War II, became a lawyer and in 1962 was appointed by President Kennedy to the United States Supreme Court where he would serve for over 30 years. In 1940, Rooney renamed the team the Pittsburgh Steelers.

Rooney married Kathleen McNulty in 1931 and they had five sons. He was involved in many businesses and political enterprises over the years, including racing and boxing, and was a partner in the General Braddock Brewing Company which made "Rooney Beer." Rooney made one reluctant venture into elective politics that got him mentioned in *Time* magazine. He was persuaded by the Republican Party to run for Allegheny County Register of Wills. He gave only one speech during the campaign. Newspaper and magazine accounts of the story report that Rooney stood up and said that he didn't know the first thing about being Register of Wills. In fact, he didn't even know where the office was located. He said he would consult the phone directory to find the office and assured voters that if he won he would hire capable assistants to run the office. He lost and never ran for office again.

One of the most amazing and convoluted deals he ever made was after the 1940 football season involving the Steelers. Rooney was tired of losing on the field and at the gate. The owner of the Philadelphia Eagles, Bert Bell (see *Keystone Tombstones Volume 2*, Chapter 3), shared those same feelings. A man named Alexis Thompson approached Bell about buying the Eagles intending to move the franchise to Boston. Bell contacted Rooney and brokered a deal in which Rooney sold the Steelers for $160,000 and invested $80,000 to become a partner in the Eagles. The sale was approved and the team was renamed the Ironmen, but the other owners refused permission for the team to leave Pennsylvania.

Rooney meanwhile had second thoughts. Thompson was a rich playboy who lived in New York and Rooney proposed that they now swap cities. Rooney and Bell would take their franchise back to Pittsburgh and renamed it the Steelers while Thompson could operate his franchise from Philadelphia and be closer to New York.

All sides agreed and from 1941 until 1946 when Bert Bell became NFL commissioner and gave up his interest in the Steelers, the teams operating name was Philadelphia Eagles Football Club Inc. The NFL considers the Rooney ownership reign unbroken because they never actually missed a game in Pittsburgh.

The Steelers had their first winning season in 1942 but then in 1943 - when the loss of players due to World War II depleted their roster - they survived by forming a merger. Rooney sought out Thompson (who was serving in the Army) and they got the NFL to approve a merger known as the Phil-Pitt Eagles-Steeler Combine. Within weeks they were dubbed the "Steagles." The two head coaches, Walt Kiesling and Earle Neale, hated each other, so Rooney had Neale coach the offense and Kiesling coached the defense. All of the players were required to keep full-time jobs in defense plants.

The Steagles finished the season 5-4-1, the first winning season in the history of the Philadelphia franchise and just the second for Pittsburgh. The team wore green and white and played six of its 10 games at "home": two at Forbes Field in Pittsburgh and four at Shibe Park in Philadelphia.

After the war, Rooney became team president and focused on trying to bring an NFL championship to Pittsburgh. He moved the Steelers' offices from the ground floor of the Fort Pitt Hotel to the fourth floor of an office building. Rooney loved to tell the story of how when the office was at the Fort Pitt Hotel, guests used to come in and leave through a window that opened onto the street instead of taking the long way around through the hotel lobby. Pie Traynor (see Chapter 27), the Pirate baseball Hall of Famer and a regular at nightly card games that were held at the Fort Pitt, refused to come to the new offices. He was sure that he would forget where he was and step out the fourth floor window some night.

Despite his efforts, the Steelers remained perennial also-rans and were known in the NFL as the "lovable losers." It did not help that they cut the then-unknown Johnny Unitas in training camp and traded their first round pick in 1965 to the Bears, who drafted Dick Butkus.

Finally, in the 1970's the team hit on the right combination of coaches and players. The Steelers became the most dominant team of an entire decade. They won four Super Bowls (1974, 1975, 1978 and 1979) during a streak of 13 consecutive winning

This plot contains the remains of Art Rooney, the owner of the Pittsburgh Steelers, who was known as "The Chief."

seasons which included an eight-year run of playoff appearances.

After the 1974 season, Rooney relinquished day-to-day operation of the Steelers and named his oldest son, Dan, president. He did, however, remain Chairman of the Board until his death. With his family at his bedside, Art Rooney died on August 25, 1988 at Mercy Hospital in Pittsburgh, eight days after suffering a stroke. He was 87 years old.

Well before the Steelers won even a single title, Art Rooney's football achievements and contributions to the game were significant enough to warrant his election into the Pro Football Hall of Fame in 1964. There are tributes to him everywhere. A large statue of his likeness, built with donations of more than $371,000 from fans, sits just outside the Steelers' current home at Heinz Field, near "Art Rooney Avenue." Duquesne University plays football at Rooney Field, and there is a Rooney Middle School on Pittsburgh's North Side. St. Vincent College (where the Steelers hold training camp each summer) and Indiana University of Pennsylvania both have dormitories named "Rooney Hall." There are numerous books about Art Rooney, as well as a one-man play called "The Chief" in which Rooney is the only character. This author has seen "The Chief," and it was a sheer delight. Art Rooney is buried at Christ Our Redeemer Catholic Cemetery (sometimes referred to as "North Side Catholic Church") on his beloved North Side of Pittsburgh.

If You Go:

Also buried in Christ Our Redeemer Cemetery is one of Art Rooney's coaches, **Walter Kiesling**. Kiesling was inducted into the Pro Football Hall of Fame for his play with a number of teams from 1926 until 1939. He coached the Steelers from 1939 to 1944 and again from 1954 to 1956. Kiesling was head coach when a young Pittsburgh-born and bred Johnny Unitas was cut at the end of training camp in 1955. Kiesling never even let Unitas take a snap in practice. After being cut, Unitas hitchhiked home and took a job as a piledriver at a construction job while continuing to play football for a semi-pro team on rock- and glass-covered fields in Pittsburgh for $6 a game. Unitas' rights were picked up the following year by the Baltimore Colts, and he went on to be one of the greatest quarterbacks ever to play.

Also buried in Christ Our Redeemer is Vietnam Medal-of-Honor recipient **John Gary Gertsch**. Staff Sergeant Gertsch was awarded the Medal of Honor for his bravery in the Republic of Vietnam's A-Shau Valley, during combat from July 15-19, 1969, when he was killed in combat.

22.
The Great American Beauty

Lillian Russell
County: Allegheny
Town: Pittsburgh
Cemetery: Allegheny Cemetery
Address: 4734 Butler Street

She was one of the most famous entertainers of the late 19th and early 20th centuries. She was known for her acting and singing. She was admired for her beauty as well as her stage presence. She was married four times with her longest relationship being with Diamond Jim Brady who allowed her to live the lifestyle she had grown accustomed to for four decades. She was often referred to as the most beautiful woman in the world. Her name was Lillian Russell.

Russell was born in Clinton, Iowa on December 4, 1860. Shortly after her birth her parents moved to Chicago where she was raised. Her father, Charles Leonard, was a newspaper publisher. Her mother was a noted feminist named Cynthia Leonard who would become the first woman to run for mayor of New York City. Growing up in Chicago she appeared in many school productions. In addition she began to study music on her own and she sang in choirs.

When she was eighteen her parents separated, and Russell moved with her mother to New York. Soon after settling in New York she joined the chorus of the Brooklyn Park Theatre. She was also taking singing lessons during this period. In 1879, she made her initial appearance on Broadway at Tony Pastor's Theatre where she was billed as an "English ballad Singer." Pastor, who many credit with being the founder of vaudeville, was known for recognizing and introducing new performers. It was Pastor who gave her a new name and set her on the path to becoming a star.

Later in 1879 she joined the touring production of Gilbert and Sullivan's "H. M. S. Pinafore. Within two weeks, she married the company's orchestra director Harry Braham after she discovered she was pregnant. She gave birth to a son who died when a nanny who was changing a diaper pierced the baby's stomach with a pin. The marriage dissolved soon after.

By 1881, she was back in Pastor's Theatre where she had a role as the leading soprano in a burlesque of the "Pirates of Penzance." During this period she appeared in a number of New York theatres. It was at the Casino Theatre in 1883 that she met the composer Edward Solomon while she was starring in a play called "Billee Taylor." In 1884 Russell and Solomon were wed about one year after the birth of their daughter who was named Dorothy Lillian Russell.

She traveled with Solomon to England where she appeared in a number of his productions including "Pocahontas" and "Polly." She was in London when she was hired to play the title role of Princess Ida in a Gilbert and Sullivan production. However during rehearsals she had disagreements with Gilbert, and he dismissed her. She

Lillian Russell

returned to the states and went on tour for Pastor appearing in comic opera's that were composed by her husband. Solomon was arrested for bigamy in 1886 since when he had married Russell he had not yet obtained a divorce from a previous marriage. Russell divorced Solomon in 1893. During this period Russell was also the companion of Diamond Jim Brady who clearly loved her. For forty years he would present her with diamonds and other gems while he supported her luxurious lifestyle.

Russell had become the most famous singer of operettas in the country. The news media touted her singing ability as well as her beauty and stage presence. The actress Marie Dressler once said of Russell, "I can still recall the rush of pure awe that marked her entrance on the stage. And then the thunderous applause that swept from orchestra to gallery, to the very roof."

It was the inventor of the telephone, Alexander Graham Bell, who introduced long distance calling in 1890. Russell singing the "Sabre Song" to listeners in Boston and Washington D. C. was the first voice heard over those telephone lines. For fun during this time frame she and her friend Diamond Jim Brady would ride bikes together in Central park. Russell's bike had been made for her by Tiffany and Company. It was a gold plated bike set with diamonds and emeralds. The bike cost $1,900.

1882 photo of Lillian Russell in the Bijou Opera House production of Gilbert and Sullivan's Patience

From 1899 to 1904 Russell starred for the Weber and Fields Music Hall. In 1902 prior to the production of "Twirly-Whirly" John Stromberg , who had already composed a number of hit songs for Russell was slow in delivering her solo for the show giving the excuse that it simply wasn't ready. A few days before the rehearsals were to begin Stromberg committed suicide. A song titled "Come Down My Evening Star" was found in one of his pockets. It would become Russell's signature song and the only one she ever recorded. She would take her place on stage in a $3,900 diamond-studded corset and deliver the number. At the time she was being paid $5,000 per week.

After leaving Weber and Fields, Russell made numerous appearances on vaudeville stages. Around this time she began having vocal problems so she started appearing in non-musical comedies. She did so until 1911 when she returned to singing in burlesque and variety theatres.

In 1912, Russell married for the fourth time. Her husband, Alexander Pollock Moore, was the owner of the Pittsburgh Leader. After her marriage she seldom

Lillian Russell

appeared on stage entering a semi-retirement stage. That same year she made her last appearance on Broadway. In 1915, she appeared in the film "Wildfire" which also starred Lionel Barrymore. She made her last appear-ance on the vaudeville stage in 1919. Ill health forced her to retire after a career that spanned four decades.

After retiring from the stage Russell wrote a newspaper column and was a strong supporter of women's rights as her mother had been. During World War 1 she aided the marines in their recruiting efforts. By this time she was a very wealthy woman, and she made a sizable donation to sponsor the formation of a Chorus Equity Association for the chorus girls of the Ziegfeld Follies.

In 1922, President Harding sent Russell to Europe on a fact finding mission to investigate the increase in immigration to the United States. She recommended a five year moratorium on immigration and some of her findings found their way into the 1924 immigration reform law. On the return trip she suffered minor injuries, which led to complications, and she died at her home in Pittsburgh ten days after her return on June 6, 1922. She was 61 years old, and she was laid to rest in Allegheny Cemetery in Pittsburgh.

If You Go:

You could spend all day touring Allegheny Cemetery. Among the people interned there are the legendary baseball player **Josh Gibson**, the noted composer **Stephen Foster** and **Harry Thaw** whose story was included in the book and movie "Ragtime" (All three have Chapters in *Keystone Tombstone Volume 2*). The great jazz saxophonist **Stanley Turrentine's** final resting place is here as well.

There are two Civil War Medal of Honor recipients, **Archibald H. Rowland Jr.** and **Alfred L. Pearson**, buried here as well. After the war, Pearson commanded the National Guardsmen who were sent to Luzerne County to quell riots in the coal region. He ordered his men to open fire on the rioters and killed a number of them. As a result he was arrested and charged with murder, but a grand jury failed to indict him, and he was set free.

In addition, you may want to visit the Arsenal Monument which is also on the cemetery's grounds. The monument honors 43 women who are buried here after an explosion at the nearby Allegheny Arsenal took their lives. The explosion was the worst industrial accident associated with the Civil War.

Here's the final resting place for a woman considered to be one of the great beauty's of her time.

Not far from the cemetery there is a great restaurant called 'Piccolo Forno." It is located at 3801 Butler Street. The eatery offers great service and terrific Italian food that is reasonably priced. It's definitely worth checking out.

Arlen Specter

23.
The Single Bullet Theory Senator

Arlen Specter
County: Montgomery
Town: Huntingdon Valley
Cemetery: Shalom memorial Park
Address: 101 Byberry Road

He was a district attorney for the city of Philadelphia. As a staff member for the Warren Commission he is largely credited with the development of the controversial single bullet theory that allowed the Commission to conclude that Lee Harvey Oswald assassinated President John F. Kennedy and that he acted alone. He represented Pennsylvania in the United States Senate for 30 years. His name was Arlen Specter.

Specter was born on February 12, 1930, in Wichita, Kansas. His parents, Harry Specter and Lillie Shanin, who were Jewish, had come to the United States from Russia, and Arlen was their youngest child. Specter's father served the United States during World War 1, and after the war he worked as a fruit peddler, a tailor and as a junkyard owner.

Specter's family moved from Wichita to Russell, Kansas where Specter graduated from Russell High School in 1947. He first attended college at the University of Oklahoma before transferring to the University of Pennsylvania. His major was international relations, and he graduated in 1951. After graduation he enlisted in the United States Air Force where he served from 1951 to 1953. It was in 1953 that he married Joan Levy. He then entered Yale University where he studied law and graduated in 1956. That same year Specter was admitted to the Pennsylvania Bar. During this time, Specter's family had moved from Kansas to Philadelphia. Specter said they made the move because his sister Shirley had reached marriageable age, and there were no other Jews in Russell.

Specter then opened the law practice of "Specter and Katz" (Marvin Katz would go on to be a Federal District Court judge in Philadelphia). In 1959 Specter went to work in the Philadelphia District Attorney's office as an assistant district attorney. He would serve in that position until 1964.

In 1964 Specter became an assistant counsel for the Warren Commission which had been established to investigate the assassination of President Kennedy. The investigation was divided into six different areas and Specter was assigned to area 1 which was "The Basic Facts of the Assassination." This area would determine the number and source of the shots. Francis Adams and Specter were placed in charge of this area. When Adams resigned in March of 1964, Specter went on to be the primary manager of this critical area. By the time Specter was finished with this job, he would have done something for which he will always be remembered, namely, the development of the single bullet theory.

Arlen Specter reproducing the assumed alignment of the single-bullet theory

Soon after it was created, the Warren Commission received a report from the FBI that indicated three shots had been fired at the Kennedy motorcade. The report went on to state that Kennedy had been hit in the back by the first shot, that Texas Governor John Connally seated in front of the president was struck by the second bullet and that the third shot hit President Kennedy in the head killing him. The FBI also concluded that the three shots originated from the 6^{Th} floor window of a building known as the Texas School Book Depository and that they had been fired by an employee there named Lee Harvey Oswald.

That was all well and good until it was discovered that a spectator in Dealey Plaza on that fateful day by the name of James Tague had been stuck by a piece of cement that came from a nearby curb after it had been hit by a bullet. Since a film of the assassination known as the Zapruder film existed, the FBI was able to determine the maximum amount of time in which the three shots could have been fired from Oswald's rifle. When the Tague shot was discovered, it was obvious that Oswald could not have fired four shots in the time allowed. Therefore to admit the existence of a fourth shot meant there had to be another shooter besides Oswald present that day in Dallas.

This is where Specter came to the rescue. He was the key figure in developing the theory that the first shot entered Kennedy in the back exited his throat and then struck Connally causing all of his wounds. So now the finding was that the first bullet wounded both Kennedy and Connally, that the second missed and hit the curb wounding Tague and the third killed Kennedy. This explanation has become known in history as the single bullet theory. Despite the fact that at least two members of the Commission never accepted the theory it was adopted and presented as what had occurred in their report to President Johnson.

When the Commission's report was made public it didn't take critics long to attack the single bullet theory. They were aided by the fact that the bullet had been found on a stretcher in Parkland hospital. They pointed out that the bullet had been fired from a high powered rifle and that if it hit the two men it caused seven wounds including shattering a rib and a wrist bone, yet it was discovered in nearly pristine condition. The critics dubbed it the "magic bullet."

Arguments over Specter's theory continue to the present day over fifty years since the assassination. New books come out on a consistent basis taking one side or the other. Specter's name will forever be associated with the theory. Specter even made it into the Oliver Stone movie "JFK." In a courtroom scene Kevin Costner, playing New Orleans District Attorney Jim Garrison, delivers a speech where he says,

"So a single bullet remained to account for all seven wounds in Kennedy and Connally. But rather than admit to a conspiracy or investigate further, the Commissioners chose to endorse the theory put forth by an ambitious junior counselor, Arlen Specter. One of the grossest lies ever forced on the American people, we've come to know it as the 'magic bullet' theory."

With his work for the Commission completed Specter, who was a registered Democrat, ran for Philadelphia District Attorney as a Republican in 1965. He beat James Crumlish, the man he used to work for and who during the campaign referred to him as "Benedict Arlen.' He would serve as Philadelphia District Attorney until 1975 when he resumed his law practice.

In 1976 Specter entered the Republican primary, along with five other candidates, in an attempt to secure the nomination to run for the United States Senate. He finished second losing to John Heinz who went on to win the general election. In 1978 he ran for the office of Governor of Pennsylvania but was defeated in the Republican primary by Dick Thornburgh. In 1980 Specter ran yet again for a seat in the United States Senate, and this time he was successful. He took office in 1981. It was a seat he would hold for thirty years.

As a Senator he took an active interest in foreign affairs and met with many foreign leaders. He was a strong supporter of appropriations used to fight the global AIDS epidemic. He also backed free trade agreements between the United States and underdeveloped countries. He also worked with local leaders from his state to help them secure federal aid and grants. During his time in office Specter brought more financial resources to Pennsylvania than any other politician. Still, as a Senator, he is probably best remembered for the work he did on the Senate Judiciary Committee which he chaired from 2005 to 2007.

As a member of the Judiciary Committee, Specter participated in the confirmation hearings of 14 Supreme Court nominees. His actions with regard to two of these nominees stand out. Of course, we're talking about Robert Bork and Clarence Thomas.

On July 1, 1987, President Ronald Reagan nominated Robert Bork to fill a vacancy on the Supreme Court. Within 45 minutes of the nomination Senator Ted Kennedy took the Senate floor and declared,

"Robert Bork's America is a land in which women would be forced into back-alley abortions, blacks would sit at segregated lunch counters, rogue police could break down citizens doors in midnight raids, schoolchildren could not be taught about evolution, writers and artists could be censored at the whim of the government and the doors of the federal courts would be shut on the fingers of millions of citizens."

It was clear that there was going to be a real fight over this nomination. Specter became one of the leaders in the fight against the Senate confirmation of Bork. On October 6, 1987, the Judiciary Committee voted 9 to 5 to send Bork's nomination to the Senate floor with an unfavorable recommendation. Specter was the only Republican on the committee voting with the majority. On October 23, 1987, the Senate rejected Bork's nomination by a vote of 58 to 42. Conservative Republicans would never forgive Specter for his position relative to Bork's nomination.

After his defeat, Bork claimed that Specter came into the hearings with his mind made up. Specter denied the charge saying he spent two weeks reading all of Bork's speeches and his opinions. As a matter of fact Specter said, "I knew more about his record than he did."

On July 1, 1991, President George Bush nominated Clarence Thomas to fill a vacancy on the Supreme Court. His confirmation hearings before the Judiciary Committee were televised and captured the attention of the nation. A woman, named Anita Hill, testified that when she worked for Thomas at the Department of Education he repeatedly talked about sex and pornographic films. Specter was Hill's harshest questioner and many felt that his approach inflamed racial and gender divisions. Thomas was eventually confirmed by a vote of 52 to 48 with Specter voting yes. Specter would later say that his aggressive questioning almost cost him his Senate seat in the election of 1992.

In that election a political novice a woman by the name of Lynn Yeakel entered the Democrat primary seeking the party's nomination to run against Specter. She was given little chance. She ignored her primary opponents and decided to run against Specter from the start. She said that Specter's questioning of Anita Hill showed an absolute disrespect for women. Her strategy worked, and she came from nowhere to win the primary. In the general election, which was bitterly contested, Specter won by just over two percentage points.

In June of 1993, Specter faced the first of several serious health problems he would battle late in his life. He had a brain tumor removed at the University of Pennsylvania Hospital in Philadelphia. On that same day, Pennsylvania's Governor Bob Casey (See Chapter 5) underwent a double-organ transplant receiving a new heart and liver at the University of Pittsburgh Medical Center. Specter had tumors removed again in 1996, and then in 1998 he underwent open heart surgery.

As evidenced by his vote not to confirm Robert Bork, Specter was not afraid to go against the wishes of the Republican Party. In 1998 and 1999, Specter criticized his party for impeaching President Bill Clinton. When his turn came to vote on impeaching the President, Specter cited Scots law and rendered a verdict of not proven. The Senate recorded his vote as not guilty. He voted in favor of the Iraq war and was a strong supporter of embryonic stem cell research.

Despite his years of service Specter, as the Republican Party became more conservative, was viewed as a RINO meaning a Republican in name only. In 2004, a conservative Pennsylvania Congressman named Pat Toomey challenged Specter in the

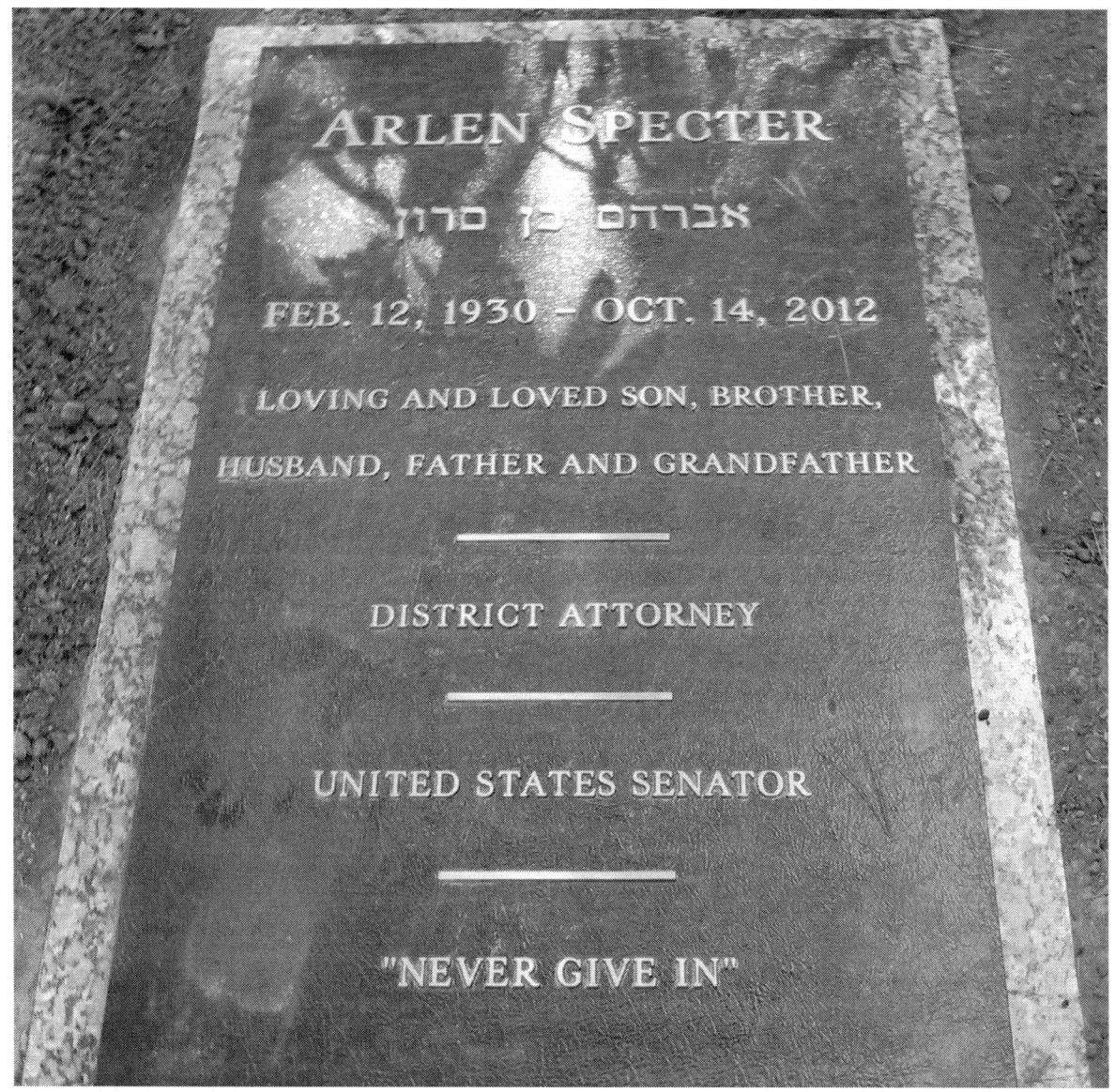

This is the grave of the man who championed the single bullet theory while a member of the Warren Commission.

Republican primary. Toomey had strong conservative support and financial backing. Specter won the primary by just 1.6 percent.

After that election, Specter once again angered conservative Republicans when he said,

"When you talk about judges who would change the right of a woman to choose, overturn Roe v. Wade, I think confirmation is unlikely. The president is well aware of what happened, when a number of his nominees were sent up, with the filibuster...And I would expect the president to be mindful of the considerations I am mentioning."

Conservative groups interpreted this as a warning and some even a threat to President Bush.

Specter even got involved in a Super Bowl controversy. During the 2007-2008 NFL season, Specter wrote to the league's commissioner Roger Goodell. Specter was interested in the destruction of the New England Patriots Spygate tapes, and he questioned whether the tapes were tied to the Patriots Super Bowl victory over the Philadelphia Eagles. Goodell responded that the tapes had been destroyed because they confirmed what he already knew. Specter then made a public statement calling for the NFL to initiate a Mitchell type investigation. Specter stated, "I have been careful not to call for a Congressional hearing because I believe the NFL should step forward and embrace an independent inquiry and Congress is extraordinarily busy on other matters. If the NFL continues to leave a vacuum, Congress may be tempted to fill it."

In March of 2009, one year before he would again seek reelection, the political columnist John Baer suggested that it was time for Specter to "come home" to the Democratic Party. Specter stated that he had no intention of doing so. Pat Toomey was likely to challenge him in the Republican primary again, and polls showed him beating Specter easily. Specter, seeing the writing on the wall, announced he was switching parties in April of 2009. The switch provided Democrats with a sixty seat filibuster proof majority in the Senate.

Becoming a Democrat did not save Specter from a primary challenge in 2010. A Congressman from suburban Philadelphia named Joe Sestak decided to run against Specter. Few gave Sestak any chance of beating Specter, but he ran an aggressive and tireless campaign. When the votes were counted, Sestak won the primary taking 53.9 percent of the vote. Sestak went on to lose the general election to Toomey.

After leaving the Senate, Specter became an adjunct professor at the University of Pennsylvania Law School. He taught a course on the relationship between Congress and the Supreme Court. The "National Jurist" named him as one of the 23 professors to take before you die.

In 2005, Specter announced that he had been diagnosed with an advanced form of Hodgkin's lymphoma, a type of cancer. In 2012 he was hospitalized, and it was announced that he was battling cancer. After he was released from the hospital, he returned home where he died on October 14, 2012. He was 82 years old. President Obama ordered United States flags to be lowered to half staff upon hearing of Specter's death.

If You Go:

The authors highly recommend a stop at Miller's Ale House located at 2300 Easton Road in Willow Grove. Miller's features a wide variety of draft beers and a menu that appeals to all tastes. In addition the servers are friendly and eager to meet your every need.

24.
Titanic Victims and Survivors

41°43.5' N 49°56.8' W
15 April 1912

For more than 100 years, the story of the sinking of the RMS *Titanic* has fascinated people all over the world. On the night of April 14 and the morning of April 15, 1912, four days into her maiden voyage, the largest passenger liner in the world hit an iceberg and sunk in the icy North Atlantic Ocean. Two hours and forty minutes after hitting the iceberg, she disappeared beneath the sea. She was carrying an estimated 2,224 people from Southampton, England to New York City, 1,500 of whom lost their lives in the tragedy, making it one of the deadliest peacetime maritime disasters in history.

Once the British passenger liner hit the iceberg and started taking on water, much chaos ensued and many controversies have endured for over a century. The evacuation was chaotic and controversial. Those who survived were rescued by the RMS *Carpathia*, which arrived about an hour and a half after the sinking. Less than a third of those aboard survived the disaster. Some survivors died shortly afterwards from injuries or the effects of exposure. Statistics compiled after the disaster show that 49% of the children and 26% of the female passengers died. The percentages for male passengers and crew were 82% and 78%, respectively. However, the figures show stark differences in the survival rates of the different classes. Only 3% of first-class women were lost, but 54% of those in third class died. Similarly, five of six first-class and all second-class children survived, but 52 of the 79 in third class perished. The figures for men show one-third of first-class men were saved but only 8% and 16% of second- and third-class men survived, respectively.

As the great ship went down, over a thousand passengers and crew members were still on board. Hundreds more were left dying in the icy 28°F sea, due to insufficient lifeboats and an inefficient, chaotic evacuation. Most lifeboats had empty seats. As the occupants sat and watched the horror around them, they could hear those freezing to death in the water as they yelled, screamed and pled for their lives.

Only a few of those in the water survived. Occupants of the lifeboats debated and argued about attempting to help those in the water. In all but two of the boats the occupants decided against trying to help, fearing that they would be capsized by the desperate, panicked swimmers. After about 20 minutes, the cries for help began to fade as the swimmers lapsed into unconsciousness and died. One of the *Titanic's* officers in Lifeboat No. 14 gathered together five of the lifeboats and transferred the occupants between them to free up space and headed back to the site of the sinking. Almost all of those in the water were already dead. They found four men still alive, one of whom died shortly afterwards. The *Carpathia* took the survivors to New York where the full scope of the disaster was just becoming known.

For years after, controversies and investigations would ensue. Issues like the speed and course of the *Titanic*, the failure to heed six warnings, the insufficient number of

RMS Titanic sea trials, April 2, 1912

lifeboats, the chaotic evacuation, poor radio communication between ships at sea, and the survival of J. Bruce Ismay, managing director of the White Star Line (owner of the *Titanic*) who was aboard, were just a few of the subjects that came under close scrutiny following the disaster.

Pennsylvania, while welcoming home its share of *Titanic* survivors, also shared in the grief and sorrow of this horrible event. These are the remarkable stories of several such Pennsylvanians.[1]

Austin Van Billiard (35)
James Van Billiard (10)
Walter Van Billiard (9)

County: Montgomery
Town: Flourtown
Cemetery: Union Cemetery of Whitemarsh
Address: 654 Bethlehem Pike

Imagine the shock and despair of James Van Billiard and his wife, who learned in several days after the accident that their son Austin Van Billiard and two of their grandsons - James (age 10) and Walter (age 9) - were passengers on the *Titanic* and were missing.

Austin had been working in the diamond mining industry in South Africa for 10 years, living there with his wife and four children. During that time he was not able to see his brother or parents, who lived in Pennsylvania (North Wales Borough, Montgomery County). After much success, Austin decided to return to the U.S. to be a diamond merchant there. The family left South Africa and on their way to America they stopped to visit his wife's parents who lived in London. Austin then decided to take his two eldest sons with him ahead of the rest of the family for a surprise visit. He took with him at least 12 uncut diamonds - diamonds which would soon be found on his body when it was recovered from the icy Atlantic.

This monument marks the final resting place of two Titanic victims the Van Billiards Austin, and his son James. Another son named Walter also perished but his body was never found.

The senior Van Billiards received a cablegram from their daughter-in-law informing them that Austin and the boys were on the *Titanic*. It was the first they knew of it.

Austin's body and that of his son Walter were recovered. James' body was never found (or, if it was recovered, was never identified). The family speculates that the boys would not have left their father to get on a lifeboat. The bodies of Austin and Walter are buried in Union Cemetery in Whitemarsh, Montgomery County. The headstone also lists James.

---

1 A number in parenthesis after an individual's name in each heading indicates that person's age at the time he or she perished on April 14-15, 1912. If no number is present after a person's name, that indicates the person survived the disaster.

William Loch Coutts
County: Allegheny
Town: Penn Hills
Cemetery: Sunset View Cemetery
(a/k/a, Riverview Memorial Park)
Address: 2023 Lincoln Road

Unlike the Van Billiards, the situation was different for two other little boys who accompanied a parent aboard the *Titanic*. Mrs. Winnie "Minnie" Coutts and her two sons, William (age 9) and Neville (age 3) were third-class passengers on the *Titanic* heading to be reunited with her husband who was working in Brooklyn as an engraver. He had been sending money to Winnie for a year to pay for the trip.

The night of the disaster, she was awakened by the commotion outside her stern cabin. She dressed her boys but found only two life preservers in her cabin. She put them on her boys and entered the hallway. She quickly found herself lost but soon encountered a crewman who gave her his life preserver and directed her up to the lifeboats, all the while asking her to pray for him if she was saved. After finding their way to the boat deck, Winnie and her sons encountered a problem: the officer in charge of the lifeboat refused to let Willie board because he looked too old. Apparently the straw hat he was wearing made him look older. Nevertheless, Winnie finally persuaded the officers to let the 9-year old join her and Neville in Lifeboat No. 2. All three Coutts were picked up by the *Carpathia*. There were only 17 in the lifeboat, which was designed to hold at least 40-60 people.

Life As *Titanic* Survivors: The family moved to Pittsburgh in 1920, and Mrs. Coutts and Neville moved to California about 20 years later. William became a professional musician, got married, and had two daughters. On Christmas Day 1957, he was found dead in the street in Steubenville, Ohio. His death was attributed to natural causes. He is buried at Sunset View Cemetery in Penn Hills Township near Pittsburgh. He was 55 years old.

His mother, Winnie, died in New Jersey in 1960, at the age of 84.

On December 16, 1958, his brother Neville was one of a dozen or so *Titanic* survivors who attended the New York City premiere of the movie "A Night to Remember" (a 1958 British drama film adaptation of Walter Lord's 1955 book *A Night to Remember*, which recounts the *Titanic's* fateful final night). Neville died in Florida in 1977, at the age of 78.

Victorine Chaudanson
County: Delaware
Town: Springfield
Cemetery: Saints Peter and Paul Cemetery
Address: 1600 S. Sproul Road

At the Philadelphia premiere of "A Night to Remember," a woman named Victorine Chaudanson was honored. Miss Chaudanson was a maid for the Ryersons, a wealthy Philadelphia family, and was traveling with them on the *Titanic*. Arthur Ryerson, along with his wife (Emily) and their children (Emily, John and Suzette), were hurrying back to the U.S. after learning of the death of their son, Arthur Jr., who died in a car accident at the age of 20. Mr. Ryerson gave Victorine his life preserver when he saw that she had none. She and Mrs. Ryerson and the children were rescued in Lifeboat No. 5. Mr. Ryerson was lost in the sinking.

Life As a *Titanic* Survivor: Victorine Chaudanson later became Mrs. Henry Perkins and lived in Ridley Park, Pennsylvania. She died on August 13, 1962 (age 87), and is buried as Victorine Perkins at Saints Peter and Paul Cemetery in Springfield, Delaware County.

The grave of Victorine Chaudanson a woman who survived the sinking.

Sophie Halaut Abraham
County: Westmoreland
Town: Greensburg
Cemetery: Westmoreland County Memorial Park
Address: 150 Eastside Drive & West Newton Road (Rt. 136)

Another survivor, 18-year old Sophie Halaut Abraham, was returning from Syria where she was visiting family, witnessed some panic. When she arrived near the lifeboats, men were fighting for an opportunity to get in. Several of the ships' officers had to command them to stand back and make way for the women and children. The first sailor who tried to help Mrs. Abraham into the lifeboat lost his grip on her, and she was tossed into the sea. She was lucky enough to be taken into a crowded lifeboat, but those fortunes quickly changed when that lifeboat was upset by a big wave, dumping everyone on board into the water. Yet another lifeboat picked Mrs. Abraham and a few others out of the water. Four sailors in her lifeboat rowed away from the *Titanic* to safety.

Life As a *Titanic* Survivor: Sophie returned to Greensburg, Pennsylvania, where she lived until her death in December 1976, at the age of 82. She is buried in Westmoreland County Memorial Park in Greensburg.

Lily Potter
Olive (Potter) Earnshaw
County: Philadelphia
Town: Philadelphia
Cemetery: Laurel Hill Cemetery
Address: 3822 Ridge Avenue

Things went relatively smoothly for Lily Potter and the two passengers who accompanied her aboard the *Titanic*: her daughter (Olive Earnshaw); and her friend (Margaret Hays). Olive was going through a divorce and Lily, now a widow, thought a vacation would be good for her. They invited Margaret to join them. After touring Italy and the Middle East, they booked passage home on another ship. However, after hearing about the *Titanic* and how grand it would be to sail on her, they changed their reservations. Following the collision with the iceberg, Olive and Margaret went to see what had happened. They returned to their cabin and reported to Lily that a steward had told them not to worry and to go back to bed. Lily was upset and did not believe the steward. They dressed quickly and warmly and were put on the first lifeboat launched. All three survived in Lifeboat No. 7.

Life As *Titanic* Survivors: Lily and Olive spent the rest of their lives as huge supporters of the Red Cross. Lily helped found the Southeastern Pennsylvania Chapter of the American Red Cross. She received the Gimbel Award as Philadelphia's outstanding woman in 1939 and gave the $1,000 prize to the Red Cross. She died in January 1954, at the age of 98. Olive remarried and had two sons. She was a Red Cross volunteer for the rest of her life, which ended when she died of cancer in 1958 (age 69). Olive and Lily are buried together at Laurel Hill Cemetery in Philadelphia.

Benjamin Guggenheim

Benjamin Guggenheim (46)
Died at sea
Atlantic Ocean (375 miles South of Newfoundland,
and 963 miles northeast of New York City)
Aboard RMS *Titanic*
Body never recovered

"Women and children first!" was the order, but as the situation became more obvious and more desperate, there was some not-so-noble behavior. Many men, however, did act heroically in the face of death. One such notable person was Benjamin Guggenheim, a fabulously wealthy industrialist from Philadelphia. He was traveling with his mistress, a French singer named Leontine Aubart. He went to the boat deck and helped Aubart and her maid into Lifeboat No. 9 (both of whom survived), and then helped other women and children into lifeboats. Once they were loaded, Guggenheim and his valet, Victor Giglio, returned to their cabin and changed into evening wear. Guggenheim was heard to say "we've dressed up in our best and are prepared to go down like gentlemen." He then told a steward:

"If anything should happen to me, tell my wife in New York that I've done my best in doing my duty. No woman shall be left aboard because Ben Guggenheim was a coward."

Guggenheim and Giglio were last seen seated in deck chairs in the foyer of the Grand Staircase, sipping brandy and smoking cigars. The steward survived and delivered the message to Mrs. Guggenheim. Benjamin Guggenheim and Victor Giglio went down with the ship. Their bodies were never recovered. Guggenheim was one of the most prominent Americans lost in the disaster and has been depicted in numerous movies about the *Titanic*.

William C. Dulles (39)
County: Philadelphia
Town: Philadelphia
Cemetery: Laurel Hill Cemetery
Address: 3822 Ridge Avenue

Another prominent Philadelphian who perished in the disaster was William C. Dulles, a relative of long time CIA director John Foster Dulles, and a prominent Philadelphia lawyer in his own right. Dulles, a bachelor, had been traveling with his mother in Europe. His body was recovered by the Cable Ship (CS) *MacKay-Bennett*, and he was buried at Laurel Hill Cemetery. He was 39.

Henry Blank
County: Delaware
Town: Drexel Hill
Cemetery: Arlington Cemetery
Address: 2900 State Road

Final resting place of William Dulles who died when the great ship went down.

Mr. Henry Blank, a successful jeweler from New Jersey, was also 39 as he sat aboard the *Titanic* en route for New York. He was traveling alone, returning from a business trip to Europe. On the night of the tragedy at the moment when the *Titanic* hit the iceberg, Blank was playing cards with two men he had befriended on the ship. Someone yelled that the ship had hit an iceberg and all three went up to the Promenade Deck to catch a look at an iceberg, but the berg had passed and was not in sight. The men returned to their game.

We will never know how lucky Blank was at cards that night, but he was extremely lucky at life. The *Titanic* came to a stop shortly after the men resumed their game and curiosity got to them. They went below to look for trouble and saw seawater entering

Here is the grave of Henry Blank, a Titanic survivor, who found a place in a lifeboat because women who were offered seating refused to leave their husbands.

the squash court. They hurried to prepare to evacuate. Blank was among the first to arrive on the starboard Boat Deck. He and his friends and the women they were traveling with were assisted into Lifeboat No. 7. It was the first lifeboat lowered into the water. Here, Blank was extremely lucky.

The Captain's order of put "women and children in and lower away" was interpreted differently by *Titanic* Officers Charles Lightoller and William Murdoch, who each took charge of a side (Lightoller the port side; Murdoch the starboard side). Lightoller took the Captain's order to mean women and children *only*; Murdoch took it to mean women and children *first*. Initially, few passengers were willing to board lifeboats. Many women refused to leave the *Titanic* without their husbands and male companions. In an effort to move the evacuation along, Murdoch allowed several men into Lifeboat No. 7. It was lowered with 28 passengers on board despite a capacity of 65. Neither officer knew the capacity of the lifeboats nor that there weren't enough lifeboats for everyone.

Blank helped row away from the sinking ship. After a while, revolver shots could be heard coming from the *Titanic*. As the massive ship began to sink, the lifeboat occupants could hear the screams and cries from those left on board.

Several hours later, Blank and the other occupants of Lifeboat No. 7 were pulled from the icy Atlantic by the *Carpathia*.

Life As a *Titanic* Survivor: Blank returned to his business and prospered for many years. He died from pneumonia on St. Patrick's Day 1949, at the age of 76. He is buried in the family plot in Arlington Cemetery, in Drexel Hill, Pennsylvania.

Richard Williams
Charles Duane Williams (51)
County: Chester
Town: Wayne
Cemetery: Old St. David's Churchyard
Address: 763 South Valley Forge Road

Mr. Charles Williams and his son, Richard, weren't quite so lucky. Charles (sometimes referred to as "C. Duane") was a lawyer originally from Radnor, Pennsylvania, and a direct descendant of Benjamin Franklin. Richard, a 21-year-old accomplished tennis player, had won the Swiss Championship while being tutored privately at a Swiss boarding school, and after playing in some summer tournaments in the U.S., would be entering Harvard in the Fall. The two men were traveling from Geneva back to the U.S.

After the collision, both men left their stateroom and encountered a steward trying to open the door of a cabin behind which a panicking passenger was trapped. The younger Williams broke through the door with his shoulder. The steward threatened to report him for damaging White Star Line property. This event inspired a scene in the 1997 film "Titanic."

The two men wandered the decks as the ship sank under them. They went to the bar and the elder Williams tried to get a steward to fill his flask with whiskey. The steward refused, stating that the bar was closed and it would be against the rules. Charles handed the flask to Richard, which remains a Williams' family heirloom.

As the *Titanic* sunk, Richard and Charles found themselves in the water - swimming for their lives. There was a loud cracking sound, and Richard turned to see

Final resting place of Richard Williams a Titanic survivor who became a tennis champion.

his father crushed by the forward smokestack as it crashed down. It almost got Richard too. The resulting wave pushed him towards a lifeboat referred to as "Collapsible A," which was upright but partly flooded as its sides had not been properly raised. Richard clung to the side for some time, as the occupants were being very careful not to take on any more water. Even after being hauled aboard, the occupants had to sit in a foot of freezing water. Many died of hypothermia during the night.

The *Carpathia* arrived near dawn. Richard Williams and those still alive in Collapsible A were lifted aboard. When a doctor on board examined Richard, the doctor recommended amputation of both legs, fearing gangrene. Williams refused permission and instead walked every two hours around the clock, hoping to save his legs.

The decision worked out well for Williams. Three days later when the *Carpathia* arrived in New York, he walked off the ship. Three months later at the Philadelphia Cricket Club, he won the U.S. Mixed Doubles Tennis Championship.

Life As a *Titanic* Survivor: "Dick" Williams (as he was sometimes referred to) continued his tennis career and entered Harvard as planned. He went on to win the U.S. Singles Championship in 1914 and again in 1916, the U.S. Men's Doubles Championship twice (1925 and 1926), and the Wimbledon Men's Championship in 1920. In 1914, he played with another *Titanic* survivor, Karl Behr (rescued on Lifeboat No. 5) on the U.S. Davis Cup team. He subsequently captained the Davis Cup team from 1921 through 1925. At the 1924 Olympics in Paris, Williams and Hazel Wightman won the gold medal in mixed doubles.

Richard Williams served with distinction in the U.S. Army during World War I and was awarded the Croix de Guerre for heroism as well as the Chevalier de la Legion d'Honneur (Legion of Honor), two of France's highest military honors.

Williams went on to be a successful investment banker in Philadelphia and for 20 years served as President of the Historical Society of Pennsylvania. He died of emphysema in 1968, at the age of 77. He is buried in Old St. David Church Cemetery in Wayne, Pennsylvania. Next to his grave is a memorial marker for his father, C. Duane Williams, whose body was never recovered.

George Dunton Widener (50)
Harry Elkins Widener (27)
Eleanor Elkins (Widener) Rice

County: Philadelphia
Town: Philadelphia
Cemetery: Laurel Hill Cemetery
Address: 3822 Ridge Avenue

Reports say that one of the people seen with C. Duane Williams during the last moments of the *Titanic* was 50-year-old George Dunton Widener, one of the wealthiest men in Philadelphia. George and his wife (Eleanor) and son (Harry) were returning from a trip to Paris, where they had gone with the intention of finding a chef for George's new Philadelphia hotel, The Ritz Carlton.

Their fate was more in line with what was expected. After the evacuation began, George and Harry escorted Eleanor to Lifeboat No. 4 and helped her in. John Jacob

The Widener mausoleum honors both George and Harry Widener, Father and son, who perished on the voyage. The wife and mother Eleanor who was a survivor was laid to rest here.

Astor IV, who was one of the richest men in the world, did the same with his wife. The men were refused entry themselves by Officer Lightoller, who launched the boat with 20 of the 60 seats unoccupied.

George and Harry died, and Eleanor was rescued by the *Carpathia*. Harry's body was never recovered. George's body was recovered by the *MacKay-Bennett*, but its condition was such that it was buried at sea. A memorial service for the two of them was held at St. Paul's Episcopal Church in Elkins Park, Pennsylvania, where stained-glass windows were dedicated in their memory.

Life As a *Titanic* Survivor: Eleanor presented Harvard University with a two million dollar library in memory of her son Harry, a 1907 Harvard graduate. She also rebuilt St. Paul's Episcopal Church as a memorial to her husband, and in 1929 gave $300,000 to the Hill School at Pottstown for a general science building in memory of Harry, a 1903 Hill School graduate.

In 1915, Mrs. Widener married explorer Dr. Alexander Hamilton Rice and traveled extensively in South America, Europe and India. In July 1937, while shopping in a Paris store, she died of a heart attack, at the age of 76.

Eleanor Elkins Rice is buried in the Widener mausoleum in Philadelphia's Laurel Hill Cemetery. Her crypt makes no mention of the *Titanic*. Harry and George Widener have cenotaphs in the mausoleum, both of which reference the ship.

William Ernest Carter
County: Montgomery
Town: Bala Cynwyd
Cemetery: West Laurel Hill Cemetery
Address: 227 Belmont Avenue

William Thornton Carter
County: Montgomery
Town: Bala Cynwyd
Cemetery: West Laurel Hill Cemetery
Address: 227 Belmont Avenue

Lucile Polk Carter Brooke
County: Berks
Town: Birdsboro
Cemetery: St. Michael's Cemetery[2]
Address: Mill & Church Streets

Lucile Carter Reeves
County: Montgomery
Town: King of Prussia
Cemetery: Valley Forge Memorial Gardens
Address: 352 South Gulph Road

Things turned out differently for the Carter clan from Philadelphia, who ironically on the night of the accident were together with the Wideners at a dinner party in honor of the ship's Captain. William Carter, 36 years old, was traveling with his wife, Lucile (also 36), and his children (11-year-old son, William, and 13-year-old daughter, Lucile). Also traveling with them were their maid (Auguste Serreplan), Mr. Carter's servant (Alexander Cairns) and his chauffeur (Charles Aldworth).

The original story was that Cairns, Aldworth, and Mr. Carter escorted his wife, two children and maid to Lifeboat No. 4. The three men then left, accompanied by George Widener, John Astor and John Thayer (see below for more on Thayer). Mrs. Carter, her son and daughter, and the maid were all rescued. The men all died, *except for Mr. Carter*. Carter escaped on the Collapsible "C" lifeboat, along with Bruce Ismay. Ismay was the President of White Star Lines, the company that owned the Titanic. In the

---
[2] Now known as the New First Baptist Church of Birdsboro

tragedy's aftermath, Ismay was savaged by both the American and British Press for deserting the ship while women and children were still on board. Some papers called him the "Coward of the Titanic." There are accounts that Ismay and the elder Carter stepped into Collapsible C at the last minute. By other accounts, Carter was swimming in the water and then picked up by the lifeboat. Whatever happened, Carter actually ended up on board the *Carpathia* before his family members. More than two hours after his arrival, his wife and children reached the *Carpathia* in Lifeboat No. 4, which Mrs. Carter had helped row.

Two years later, Mrs. Carter sued for divorce and testified that her husband had left her and their children to fend for themselves. She said that after the *Titanic* hit the iceberg at 11:40 p.m., Mr. Carter came to the stateroom, told her to get up, get herself and the children dressed, and then he essentially ... vanished. According to her, from that moment until the time she arrived at the *Carpathia* around 8:00 a.m. the next morning, she did not once see Mr. Carter.

Grave of William Ernest Carter and his son William Carter both of whom survived the sinking.

Life As *Titanic* Survivors: After the divorce, Lucile married George Brooke in 1914. She died in 1934 at the age of 58 and is buried in St. Michael's Cemetery in Birdsboro, Pennsylvania. Her tombstone reads: "Lucile Polk Brooke."

William Ernest Carter died in 1940, at the age of 65. He was buried in a huge mausoleum in West Laurel Hill Cemetery. His son, William Thornton Carter, died in 1985, at the age of 84. He was buried alongside his father.

The daughter, Lucile, married a man named Samuel J. Reeves. She died in 1962, at the age of 64. Lucile Carter Reeves is reportedly buried in Valley Forge Memorial Gardens, but when the authors visited there, the staff could not find any record of her being there.

John Borland Thayer, Jr. (49)
Marian Thayer
John B. ("Jack") Thayer III

County: Montgomery
Town: Bryn Mawr
Cemetery: Church of the Redeemer Cemetery
Address: 230 Pennswood Road

Also at that dinner party hosted by the Wideners were John and Marian Thayer of Philadelphia, along with their 17-year-old son, Jack. Mr. Thayer was the second Vice

President of the Pennsylvania Railroad. They were preparing for bed when the collision occurred. Jack at first went to investigate and returned to put on warm clothes and alert his parents. They went up to the "A" Deck where things were crowded and noisy. Jack and his parents were separated in the confusion, but John saw Marian safely into Lifeboat No. 4.

Jack encountered a friend he had met earlier that evening over coffee, Milton Long, and tried to board a lifeboat, but they were turned away because they were men. They discussed jumping overboard and swimming to a lifeboat, but decided against it for the moment.

Memorial to Marian and John Thayer who were both passengers on the great ship. Only Marian survived the voyage.

John watched as Lifeboat No. 4 was lowered and his wife, Marian, helped row away from the *Titanic*. He then joined his friends, Charles Duane Williams, George Widener, and George's son, Harry, to await their fate. His body was never recovered.

Jack and Milton had watched the last lifeboats being lowered and realized they were not full. They now felt that jumping and swimming to a boat was their best chance. At 2:15 a.m. – just minutes before the *Titanic* slipped beneath the ocean's surface – the two men along with hundreds of other passengers made their way towards the stern of the ship. As the water rushed up the sinking deck, Long and Thayer stood at the starboard rail near the second smokestack, shook hands and prepared to jump into the water, now just 12 to 15 feet below them. It was the last time the two of them would ever see each other.

It was fortunate that Jack Thayer was a stronger swimmer. He struggled in the numbing cold but ultimately did manage to successfully swim against the suction of the sinking liner. Long did not fare as well. In subsequent interviews, Jack said that although he never actually saw Long again after the two of them jumped, it was his belief that Long had "been sucked into the deck below" and drowned.

Jack swam until he reached the Collapsible "B" lifeboat, which was overturned as a result of having been improperly launched. About 35 men were clinging precariously to the hull of the capsized boat. A few of those men helped pull Jack (who by that time was too exhausted to help himself) from the frigid water. Realizing the danger to the boat of being swamped by the mass of swimmers trying to reach them, the men who had found refuge on Collapsible B slowly paddled away from them.

They drifted all night, trying to remain motionless so as not to slip off into the icy water. After daylight, Lifeboat Nos. 4 and 12 came to their aid. Thayer was so distracted trying to get into boat 12 that he did not notice his mother in boat 4 nearby. Likewise, his mother was so numbed by the cold that she did not see him either. When Lifeboat No. 12 finally was rescued by the *Carpathia*, Jack and his mother were reunited and discovered that the senior Thayer, John, had not made it.

<u>Life As *Titanic* Survivors</u>: Marian Thayer never remarried. She died on April 14, 1944, the 32nd anniversary of the disaster, at the age of 72. She is buried in the Church of the Redeemer Cemetery in Bryn Mawr, Pennsylvania.

Grave of Titanic survivor Jack Thayer who later committed suicide.

Jack Thayer went on to graduate from the University of Pennsylvania, served as a captain in the artillery during World War I, got married and had five children, and had a career in banking and finance. In 1940, he described his experiences with the *Titanic*'s sinking in vivid detail in a self-published pamphlet printed for family and friends. This paper was published again in 2012 as "A Survivor's Tale: The Titanic by John B. Thayer."

Both of Jack's sons, Edward and John the IV, enlisted in the armed forces during World War II. In October 1943, Edward was killed in action in the Pacific. Jack had survived the *Titanic,* but he could not survive the death of a son. He committed suicide on September 20, 1945. He was found in an automobile at 48th and Parkside Avenue with his wrists and throat cut. He was 50 years old. He too is buried at the Church of the Redeemer Cemetery.

Charlotte Cardeza
Thomas Cardeza

County: Montgomery
Town: Bala Cynwyd
Cemetery: West Laurel Hill Cemetery
Address: 227 Belmont Avenue

Another Pennsylvanian who survived the disaster was Mrs. Charlotte Cardeza. Her father, Thomas Drake, was a co-founder of Fidelity Insurance. Mrs. Cardeza - a lover of big-game hunting - was returning home to Germantown, Pennsylvania with her 36-year-old son (Thomas), after an African safari and a visit to Thomas' hunting reserve in Hungary. They were accompanied on board the *Titanic* by Mrs. Cardeza's personal maid (Anna Ward) and Thomas' servant (Gustave Lesueur). The Cardeza entourage brought fourteen trunks, four suitcases, and three crates of baggage. They stayed in the most expensive suite on the *Titanic*, which featured two bedrooms, a sitting room, and a private 50-foot promenade.

In a strange twist of fate, all four members of their party - including two males - were allowed to board Lifeboat No. 3, and all four were rescued by the *Carpathia*.

Life As *Titanic* Survivors: Mrs. Cardeza died on August 1, 1939, at the age of 75. She is buried in a mausoleum in West Laurel Hill Cemetery. Thomas went on to be a director of his grandfather's company, Fidelity Insurance, from 1922-1951. Thomas died in June 1952, at the age of 77, and is buried with his mother in West Laurel Hill Cemetery.

Anna Ward, who had a premonition that something bad was going to happen, had to be persuaded to make the trip by her mother. She went on to marry Mrs. Cardeza's gardener, William Moynahan. She died on Christmas Day 1955, at the age of 81, and is buried with her husband in West Laurel Hill Cemetery.

Fortunately for chocolate lovers all over the world, Milton Hershey and his wife, Kitty, who had put a $300 deposit down for tickets on the *Titanic*, did not make the journey. The Hersheys were on a lengthy trip to Nice, France, and had planned months in advance to make their return voyage home aboard the supposedly-unsinkable luxury vessel. However, urgent (and ultimately, life-saving!) business matters arose in the U.S. for which Mr. Hershey was needed. He and Kitty thus had to cancel their *Titanic* reservations and return to America a few days earlier than planned, ironically aboard the German ship, *Amerika*. They arrived back home several days before the *Titanic* sunk.

The check for the transaction, made out to White Star Lines, is still in the Hershey Community Archives. Milton Hershey is the subject of a chapter in *Keystone Tombstones: Volume 2*.

Milton Hershey c. 1905

If You Go:

We have said many times in our various volumes what treasures **Laurel Hill Cemetery** and **West Laurel Hill Cemetery** are. They contain hundreds of graves of interesting and important historical figures, many of whom are mentioned in our books.

Some other graves of interest in other cemeteries mentioned in this chapter are:

At **Old Saint David Church Cemetery**, you will find one of the graves of **Anthony Wayne** (see Chapter 29 of this volume), a Revolutionary War hero who is buried in two places.

Also at **Old Saint David Church Cemetery** is the grave of **William Atterbury**, who was vice president of the Pennsylvania Railroad when he was abruptly commissioned a Brigadier General in the United States Army during World War I. He was appointed Director General of Transportation for the Armed Services in Europe. His reorganization of the European Railroad Network contributed to the victory for the Allies. He was nicknamed "The Railroad General" and received medals from many nations, including the Distinguished Service Medal and the French Legion of Honor.

The **Church of the Redeemer Cemetery** has the grave of artist **Mary Cassatt**, who became the sole American artist at the forefront of the Impressionist movement. She is widely recognized as one of the most important figures in the development of American culture and an inspiration to a generation of women in the arts. You will also find the grave of **George Earle**, the Governor of Pennsylvania from 1935-1939, and a confidant

Morrie Rath baseball card

and advisor to President Franklin D. Roosevelt.

Three interesting sports figures can be found at **Saints Peter and Paul Cemetery**:

Danny Murtaugh, who was a major league baseball player and manager. He was named National League Manager of the Year in 1944 with the Pittsburgh Pirates. He later led the Pirates to the famous upset of the heavily-favored New York Yankees in the 1960 World Series, and won the championship again in the 1971 World Series versus the Baltimore Orioles.

John Facenda, who was a sports newscaster for WCAU-TV in Philadelphia for 25 years and the voice of NFL Films for two decades.

Jack "Blackjack" Ferrante, who played for eight seasons as a wide receiver for the Philadelphia Eagles in the 1940's, despite never having attended college. He was discovered in the sandlots of Philadelphia and wound up being named an All-Pro two times and scored 31 touchdowns over his career.

At **Arlington Cemetery** are the graves of:.

Morris "Morrie" Rath, who was a major league baseball player for the Philadelphia Athletics (1909-10), the Cleveland Naps (1910), Chicago White Sox (1912-13) and Cincinnati Reds (1919-1920). Batting leadoff for the Reds in the 1919 World Series, Rath became a key figure in the ensuing "Black Sox" scandal when he was hit by White Sox pitcher Eddie Cicotte with the second pitch of the Series. This was believed to be a signal to gamblers that the White Sox had agreed to throw the series.

Theodore Smith, who was an Indian Wars Medal of Honor recipient.

25.
Football's Jackie Robinson

Willie Thrower
County: Westmoreland
Town: Lower Burrell
Cemetery: Greenwood Memorial Park
Address: 104 Melwood Road

The next time you are gathered around the TV watching NFL football, ask other NFL fans who was the first black man to play quarterback in the NFL. It's very doubtful that you will get the answer 'Willie Thrower.' Yet Willie Thrower (could there be a better name for a quarterback?) was the first African-American player to appear in a "modern era" professional game at quarterback in the National Football League.

Thrower was born in New Kensington, Pennsylvania on March 22, 1930. That area of Pennsylvania was a crucible for forging Hall-of-Fame quarterbacks like George Blanda, Johnny Unitas, Joe Namath, Joe Montana, Jim Kelly and Dan Marino. They all played their high school football in a very small area near Pittsburgh, but none left a bigger imprint on the high school gridiron than Thrower. He made the varsity as a freshman at New Kensington High School (present-name: Valley High School), and turned a strong squad into a championship one. He played halfback in a single-wing offense on a team that would win two Western Pennsylvania titles and lose just one game in his final three years. In his senior year, he was named All-State and All-American.

His games drew a lot of attention, including from college recruiters - many of whom turned away when they discovered he was black. In 1947, the Orange Bowl actually rescinded the invitation it had extended to Valley High to play in its annual prep classic game when organizers saw a photograph of its star.

One recruiter who didn't turn away was Duffy Daugherty, the assistant coach of Michigan State University. He and head coach Biggie Munn didn't care what color Thrower was. At a time when college coaches were turning black quarterbacks into halfbacks or receivers, Munn converted Thrower into a quarterback. In 1950 (Thrower's first season of eligibility), he became the first black quarterback to play in a Big 10 game.

Although he was widely regarded as the team's top passer, Thrower competed for playing time most of his career at Michigan State with All-American quarterbacks Al Dorow and Tom Yewcic. In 1952, Thrower and Yewcic teamed up to lead the Spartans to an undefeated 9-0 season and the national championship. On October 11 of that season, Thrower had a breakout performance against Texas A&M in a nationally-televised game. He was awarded the game ball by his teammates.

He followed that game with impressive performances against Syracuse, Penn State and Indiana, and then had his finest game as a Spartan against sixth-ranked Notre

Willie Thrower

Dame. Michigan State won 21-3, with Thrower engineering two touchdown drives after stepping in for an injured Yewcic.

In the final game of the season, his teammates refused his initial play call and insisted he call a quarterback sneak and score a touchdown himself in a rout of Marquette which sealed the number one ranking for Michigan State.

These performances caught the attention of the Chicago Bears. After Thrower went undrafted in the 1953 NFL draft, the Bears offered him a one-year contract for $8,500. He signed and became the backup quarterback and roommate to future Hall-of-Famer George Blanda.

Thrower made history on October 18, 1953, when he became the first African-American quarterback to play in an NFL game. Unhappy with Blanda's play during their game that day against the San Francisco 49ers at Soldier Field, Bears coach George Halas pulled him and sent in Thrower (who completed 3 of 8 passes for 27 yards). He played in one other game that season and was released by the Bears after the season. It would be 15 years before another black quarterback would take a snap in an NFL game (1968, QB Marlin Briscoe of the Denver Broncos). Thrower played semi-pro football for three years in Canada before a separated shoulder forced him to walk away from the game at age 27.

Modest grave of the NFL's first black quarterback. We visited during a heavy rainstorm.

After his retirement from football, Thrower became a social worker in New York City and worked as a child care counselor at the Hawthorne Cedar Knolls School in Westchester County, New York. He eventually moved back to New Kensington with his wife, Mary, and their three sons.

In February 2002, Willie Thrower died of a heart attack at the age of 71. In 2006, a statue of Thrower was erected near Valley High School. That same year, when former NFL quarterback Warren Moon was inducted into the pro football Hall of Fame, he mentioned Thrower in his acceptance speech. Moon thanked Thrower for giving him inspiration during a time when few African-Americans played quarterback in the NFL. The Pro Football Hall of Fame was honored Thrower by featuring him in an exhibit on early African-American players.

"I look at it like this," Thrower told the <u>Valley News Dispatch</u> of Tarentum, Pennsylvania in 2001, "I was the Jackie Robinson of football. A black quarterback was unheard of before I hit the pros."

Willie Thrower is buried in Greenwood Memorial Park in Lower Burrell, PA in a modest grave.

If You Go:

Greenwood Memorial Park is also the site of two graves of notable people:

Eddie Adams was a Pulitzer Prize-winning photographer and photojournalist noted for portraits of celebrities and politicians, as well as his coverage of 13 wars over his 50-year career. He began during the Korean War, where he served in the United States Marine Corps as a combat photographer. He went on to win more than 500 awards for his work, including the Pulitzer Prize for breaking news photography in 1969. His most famous shot was that of a communist guerrilla being executed in a Saigon street in 1968 during the Vietnam War. His works include U.S. presidents from Richard Nixon to George W. Bush, and many prominent world figures including Pope John Paul II, Ding Xiao Ping, Anwar Sadat, Fidel Castro, Mikhail Gorbachev, Indira Gandhi and the Shah of Iran.

Adams died in New York City on September 18, 2004, from complications of ALS, also known as Lou Gehrig's disease. He was 71 years old. His legacy continues through "Barnstorm: The Eddie Adams Workshop" (a photography workshop he started in 1988). He is the subject of a 2009 documentary directed by Susan Morgan Cooper and narrated by Kiefer Sutherland, entitled *An Unlikely Weapon*.

Joe Page was a left-handed relief pitcher who played with the New York Yankees from 1944 to 1950 and with the Pittsburgh Pirates in 1954. Nicknamed "The Fireman," he became the Yankees relief ace for the 1947 and 1949 World Series championship teams. He won 14 games as a reliever along with 17 saves and a 2.15 ERA in 1947, and followed up with outstanding performances in the '47 Series (getting a save and a win). He was the first World Series Most Valuable Player. In 1949, he won 13 games and saved 27, with a 2.59 ERA, and was the winning pitcher in Game 3 of the '49 Series.

In 1980, Page died of heart failure in Latrobe, Pennsylvania. He was 62 years old.

26.
Pirates' Pride

Honus Wagner
County: Allegheny
Town: Pittsburgh
Cemetery: Jefferson Memorial Park
Address: 401 Curry Hollow Road

Pie Traynor
County: Allegheny
Town: Pittsburgh
Cemetery: Homewood Cemetery
Address: 1599 Dallas Avenue

Honus Wagner and Pie Traynor were two of the greatest players to ever play major league baseball and both played almost exclusively for the Pittsburgh Pirates.

Johannes Peter "Honus" Wagner, nicknamed "The Flying Dutchman" due to his superb speed and German heritage, is regarded by most experts as the greatest shortstop in baseball history and one of the best all-around players of all time. He was born in what is now Carnegie, Pennsylvania on February 24, 1874, to Bavarian immigrants. He was one of nine children (only five of whom lived past childhood) - all boys. As a child, he was called "Hans" and it evolved into Honus. He quit school at age 12 to help his father and brothers in the coal mines. In their spare time, he and his brothers played sandlot baseball and developed their skills to such an extent that three of his brothers would play professionally.

Wagner's older brother, Albert "Butts" Wagner, is often credited for getting Honus his first tryout. Wagner was signed by baseball scout Ed Barrow when he was 18. He played briefly in the minor leagues in 1895 and 1896. Wagner had a bulky, barrel-chested appearance and ran with a bowlegged gait but was extremely fast and powerful. His arms hung so low that Lefty Gomez once remarked, "he could tie his shoes standing up." Some major league teams were put off by his appearance, but when he led the Atlantic League in hitting with a .379 average the Louisville Colonels bought him for $2,100.

Wagner made his major league debut for Louisville in July 1897. He played center field and second base and hit .338 in 61 games. In 1898, he played first, second and third base and hit .299. He followed in 1899 with a .336 average - the first of 14 consecutive seasons hitting over .300. Following the 1899 season, the National League contracted from twelve to eight teams with the Colonels being one of the teams eliminated. Owner Barney Dreyfuss purchased half ownership in the Pirates and took Wagner with him to Pittsburgh.

Wagner was delighted that he could live at home and play baseball. He had a banner year in 1900, winning the first of eight batting championships with an average of .381. He also led the league in doubles (45), triples (22) and slugging percentage (.573) while playing right field.

In 1901, the American League began to recruit and sign National League players. The Chicago White Stockings offered Wagner $20,000 (about $500,000 in today's money) to sign but he turned it down to stay in Pittsburgh. It was also in 1901 that Wagner started playing shortstop and in 1903 it became his regular position. He hit .

Honus Wagner taking batting practice c.1910

355 that year, led the league in doubles and runs batted in, and won the first of five stolen-base titles by stealing 49.

The Pirates won the pennant in 1903 and played the Boston Americans (who wouldn't become the "Red Sox" until 1908). Much was expected from Wagner but he played poorly and hit only .222 for the series, which Boston won five games to three (using a best-of-nine format). His poor performance was accentuated by unmerciful heckling from a group of Boston fans called the "Royal Rooters," who were led by Boston bartender Michael "Nuf Ced" McGreevy. They even traveled to Pittsburgh to heckle and taunt him there.

Wagner was distraught by his performance. He refused to send his picture to a "Hall of Fame" for batting champions, citing his play in the World Series. He wrote back that he would be ashamed to have his picture up. Baseball great Christy Mathewson published a book called *Pitching in the Pinch* in which he wrote the following:

For some time after Hans Wagner's poor showing in the world's series of 1903 ... it was reported that he was "yellow" (poor in the clutch). This grieved the Dutchman deeply, for I don't know a ball player in either league who would assay less quit to the ton than Wagner ... This was the real tragedy in Wagner's career. Notwithstanding his stolid appearance, he is a sensitive player, and this has hurt him more than anything else in his life ever has.

Wagner was fortunate to get another World Series opportunity in 1909 against the Detroit Tigers and Ty Cobb. Both had led their leagues in hitting, and it was the first time batting champions of each league faced each other. Wagner set a Series record by stealing six bases. The Pirates won the Series four games to three, with Wagner's triple breaking open the deciding seventh game, and he outhit Cobb .333 to .231.

After that season, the American Tobacco Company put Wagner's picture on its baseball cards as part of a tobacco promotion (referred to as the "T206 series"). The card was recalled almost immediately at the request of Wagner, who objected because he did not want to set a bad example for children. Fewer than 75 authentic 1909 Honus Wagner cards are known to exist.

In 1905, Wagner did sign a contract to produce the first bat with a player's signature, the Louisville Slugger. He is believed to be the first sportsperson to endorse a commercial product.

In 1916, he married Bessie Raine Smith, and they had three daughters. He retired in 1917 after an abbreviated season as the National League's all-time hit leader with 3,430 hits (a record which Ty Cobb would overtake in 1923). He played 21 seasons and won eight National League batting titles - a record he shares with Tony Gwynn. He batted above .300 for 17 consecutive seasons, including seven times over .350, and finished with a lifetime average of .329. He led the league five times in stolen bases, five times in RBI, eight times in doubles, and three times in triples.

After retirement, Wagner was a Pirate coach for 39 years, most notably as a hitting instructor from 1933 to 1952. Future Hall of Famers Arky Vaughan, Ralph Kiner and Pie Traynor were notable "pupils" of Wagner. He also coached baseball and basketball at what is now Carnegie Mellon University and ran for Allegheny County sheriff in 1928 but lost (he would later be appointed deputy sheriff in 1942). He served for a short time as sergeant-at-arms for the Pennsylvania legislature.

In 1936, Wagner was part of what was known as the "Fabulous Five," the first class elected to the Baseball Hall of Fame. Wagner, along with Ty Cobb, Babe Ruth, Christy Mathewson and Walter Johnson, were the distinguished members of that class.

This simple grave marks the final resting place of Honus Wagner who along with players like Ty Cobb and Babe Ruth was among the first group of inductees into the Baseball Hall of Fame.

Wagner was tied for second with Ruth in the voting (Ty Cobb received the most votes).

A life-size statue of Wagner was placed outside Forbes Field in 1955. Wagner, although then 81 and frail, was nonetheless able to attend the dedication ceremony and wave to his many fans. The Pirates have relocated twice since then, and the statue has come along with them each time. It now stands outside the main gate of PNC Park.

Honus Wagner died in Pittsburgh on December 6, 1955, and is buried in an extremely modest grave in Jefferson Memorial Park in Pleasant Hills.

In 2001, baseball historian Bill James named Wagner as the second best player of all time (after Babe Ruth), and statisticians John Thorn and Pete Palmer rated Wagner as ninth all-time in 1997. In 1999, Wagner was voted the top shortstop and 13th overall on the *Sporting News* list of the top 100 Greatest Players.

Wagner's 1909 T206 baseball card is considered the "Mona Lisa" of baseball cards, and in 2007 a mint condition card sold for $2.8 million. In 2013 another sold at auction for $2.1 million.

A sporting goods store in Pittsburgh bearing his name closed in 2011 after operating for 93 years.

Another source of Pirate Pride is one of the greatest third basemen of all time, **Harold Joseph "Pie" Traynor**. Born near Boston in 1898 to parents who had immigrated to the United States from Canada, Traynor and his family relocated to Somerville, Massachusetts when he was five years old. He loved baseball and constantly nagged the older boys to let him in their games. When they finally did relent, they put the then six-year old Traynor at catcher - without a mask. In his first game, a pitch smacked him in the mouth and knocked out two teeth.

An owner of a local corner store loved baseball and watching the young boys play the sport. When the boys came in after a game for a treat, the owner would ask what they wanted. Traynor always asked for a slice of pie. The store owner dubbed him "Pie Face" and his friends took to calling him "Pie."

He tried to enlist in the Army in 1917 but was turned down. He wanted to help in the war effort and so took a job in Nitro, West Virginia as a "car checker." His duties put him on horseback all day checking the arrival and departure of freight cars loaded with explosives.

Pie Traynor

Farrell and Farley

After the war, a scout for the Boston Braves invited Traynor to the field for a tryout. Unfortunately, the scout forgot to notify the Braves' manager, George Stallings, who proceeded to run Traynor off the field. He was later offered a spot with the Portsmouth Truckers of the Virginia League, where he impressed a Pittsburgh scout. He made his major league debut as a Pirates shortstop in September 1920. He played in 17 games and had many defensive problems. He spent most of 1921 with the Birmingham Barons, where he hit .336 and stole 47 bases but was still a defensive mess.

Traynor became the Pirates regular third baseman in 1922. His defense improved thanks to the tutoring of teammate Rabbit Maranville and he began using a heavier bat on the advice of Rogers Hornsby. It apparently paid off because in 1923 Traynor hit .338 and drove in 101 runs. The heavier bat changed Traynor from a dead pull hitter and he began spraying line drives to all fields. His defense became so good he led the league's third basemen in assists three times, putouts seven times and double plays four times. His arm was extremely strong but a little erratic. To compensate he would throw quickly so the first baseman had time to get off the bag if necessary, take the throw and get back on again.

In 1925, the Pirates won the pennant, Traynor hit .320 with 106 runs batted in, and he led the league in fielding percentage. His 41 double plays set a National League record for third basemen that stood for 25 years. He was only 26 years old. In the 1925 World Series, the Pirates beat the Washington Senators in seven games. Traynor hit .346 including a homer off of future Hall-of-Famer Walter Johnson, and gave a virtuoso performance at third base.

The Pirates won the pennant again in 1927, with Traynor hitting .342 and driving in 106 runs. The American League pennant was won by the Yankees and their feared "Murderers' Row" lineup. The 1927 Yankees team is widely considered to be one of the best baseball teams in history, and they easily defeated the Pirates in the World Series four games to none. Traynor was a non-factor.

In 1928, Traynor hit .337 and drove in a career high 124 runs. In 1930, he hit a career high .366. His last full season was 1934 when he hit over .300 for the ninth time in 10 seasons. During the 1934 season, Traynor became the Pirates player-manager. He played his final game on August 14, 1937, but stayed on as manager through the 1939 season.

His career totals over 17 seasons include 2,416 hits, a career batting average of .320 and 1,273 runs batted in. He hit over .300 ten times and drove in over 100 runs in seven seasons. He never struck out more than 28 times in a season and in 1929 struck out only seven times in 540 at bats.

After spending time as a scout for the Pirates, Traynor took a job as sports director for KQV radio in Pittsburgh. His radio broadcasts became popular, and he remained in

Here is the spot where the Hall of Fame Pittsburgh Pirate third baseman was laid to rest.

that job for 21 years. Having never learned to drive, he walked the 10-mile round trip to the station each day.

In 1948, Traynor was the first third baseman to be selected to the Baseball Hall of Fame.

In the 60's, he broadcast wrestling and became a pitchman for the American Heating Company. He became well known for the tagline "Who Can? American!" In 1969, as part of the observance of the centennial of professional baseball, Traynor was selected as the third baseman on Major League Baseball's all-time team.

Pie Traynor died of emphysema (due to smoking) on March 6, 1972. He is buried in Homewood Cemetery. There is a well-written biography by James Forr and David Proctor titled *Pie Traynor: A Baseball Biography*, which was published in 2010.

If You Go:

Jefferson Memorial Park and Homewood Cemetery are both beautiful and well-maintained cemeteries with many graves of noteworthy people.

Jefferson Memorial Park contains the graves of:

Pie Traynor's teammate, **Steve Swetonic**, who pitched for the Pirates from 1929 to 1935; famous anchorman, newsman and Pirate announcer **Paul Long**; and Korean War Congressional Medal of Honor recipient **John Doran Kelly**.

Homewood Cemetery is a treasure of historical graves from all walks of life, including:

... from the sports world: legendary University of Pittsburgh and Steeler football coach **Jock Sutherland**; Major League Baseball umpire **Charlie Williams**, who in 1993 became the first African-American umpire to work behind home plate in a World Series; and **Chuck Cooper**, a basketball star for Duquesne University and the first African-American to be drafted by an NBA team. He was drafted in the second round of the 1950 NBA draft by Red Auerbach and played six seasons in the NBA, including his first four with the Boston Celtics.

... from the science world: **Henry Koenig**, who gained world acclaim for his research with radium.

... from the music world: **Erroll Garner**, who was a famous jazz pianist and composer.

... from the political world: Senator **Henry John Heinz III** who, along with his great-grandfather (below) and other family members, is interred in the Heinz family mausoleum.

... from the business world: **Henry John Heinz**, the ketchup magnate; **Henry Clay Frick**, the "Coke King"; and **David L. Clark**, of Clark Bar and Zagnut fame.

These are just some of the interesting people buried at Homewood Cemetery.

John Updike

27.
One of America's Best

John Updike
County: Berks
Town: Plowville
Cemetery: Robeson Lutheran Church Cemetery
Address: Morgantown Road (PA State Route 10) & Plow Road

John Updike was a major American writer. He was a leading novelist who twice won the Pulitzer Prize, a poet, a short story writer, an art critic and a literary critic. He published more than 20 novels and more than a dozen short story collections, in addition to 10 poetry books and many other essays and articles. He is one of only three authors to win the Pulitzer Prize for Fiction more than once (along with Booth Tarkington and William Faulkner).

John Hoyer Updike was born on March 18, 1932, in Reading, Pennsylvania. He spent his first years in nearby Shillington. He was the only child of Wesley Russell Updike, a junior high school math teacher, and Linda Grace Hoyer Updike, an aspiring writer who later in life published short stories in *The New Yorker* and elsewhere. When he was 13, the family moved to his mother's birthplace, a stone farmhouse on an 80-acre farm near Plowville, 11 miles from Shillington where he continued to attend school. At home, his mother encouraged him to write and draw, and the isolation is thought to have stimulated his imagination. He excelled in school and served as president and co-valedictorian of his graduating class at Shillington High School. He worked as a copyboy for the *Reading Eagle* during the summers and wrote several feature stories for the newspaper.

He received a full scholarship to Harvard, where he majored in English and was a prolific contributor to the "Harvard Lampoon" as a writer and cartoonist. He also worked as an editor of the "Lampoon," and served as its president before graduating *summa cum laude* in 1954.

The year before, he had married Mary Pennington, a Radcliffe art student, and after graduating the couple moved to London, England, where Updike had won a Knox fellowship at Oxford University's Ruskin School of Drawing and Fine Art. His early ambition was to be a cartoonist.

In October 1954, a short story written by Updike appeared in *The New Yorker* magazine. The story was titled "Friends from Philadelphia," and Updike called it "the ecstatic breakthrough of my literary life." While they were in England, their first daughter, Elizabeth, was born. Upon returning to the United States, Updike settled in Manhattan in 1955 and took a job as a staff writer at *The New Yorker* at the invitation of famed editor E.B. White. He worked at *The New Yorker* writing "Talk of the Town" pieces, editorials, reviews and submitting poetry and short stories to the magazine. After the arrival of his son, David, in 1957, Updike left New York for Ipswich, Massachusetts. He continued to contribute to *The New Yorker* but resolved to support

Updike, shown here circa 1955, published his first short story in The New Yorker when he was 22.

his family by writing full time, without taking a salaried position. He maintained a lifelong relationship with *The New Yorker*, where many of his poems, reviews and short stories appeared, but he resided in Massachusetts for the remainder of his life. He must have been quite confident since he had another son (Michael) in 1959, and a daughter (Miranda) in 1960.

He quickly began his remarkable, prolific career by publishing his first volume of poetry, *The Carpentered Hen*, in 1958, followed by his first novel (*The Poorhouse Fair*) and first collection of stories (*The Same Door*) in 1959. His early stories and novels are set in the small town of Olinger, Pennsylvania, a suburb of Brewer. These settings are Shillington's and Reading's respective fictional counterparts.

Updike's career and reputation were nurtured and enhanced by his long association with *The New Yorker*, which published him frequently and provided a wonderful outlet for his short stories and poetry. He published eight volumes of poetry over his career, which has been praised for its engagement with "a variety of forms and topics," its "wits and precision," and for its depiction of topics familiar to American readers.

Although Updike's reputation rests on his complete body of work, he was first established as a major American writer upon publication of his novel *Rabbit, Run* in 1960. *Rabbit, Run* featured the character Harry ("Rabbit") Angstrom, who would become Updike's most endearing and critically acclaimed character through three additional novels. He first appears in *Rabbit, Run* as a former high school basketball star trapped in a loveless marriage and a sales job he hates. Through these four novels - *Rabbit, Run*, *Rabbit Redux*, *Rabbit is Rich* and *Rabbit at Rest* - Updike traces the funny, restless and questing life of this middle-American against the background of major events in the last half of the 20th century. In 2005, *Time* magazine featured *Rabbit, Run* in their listing of "All-Time 100 Greatest Novels."

Rabbit Redux was published in 1971 and *Rabbit is Rich* in 1980. *Rabbit is Rich* won the National Book award, the National Book Critics Circle award, and the Pulitzer Prize for Fiction - all three American literary prizes. *Rabbit at Rest* was published ten years later in 1990, and won the Pulitzer Prize and the National Book Critics Circle award.

The quartet of *Rabbit* novels established Updike's character, Rabbit Angstrom, as one of the major American literary figures along with Huckleberry Finn, Jay Gatsby and Holden Caulfield. A 2002 list by *Book* magazine of the 100 Best Fictional Characters since 1900 listed Rabbit as number five.

In 1963, Updike received the National Book Award for his novel *The Centaur*, which was inspired by his childhood in Pennsylvania. The following year, at age 32, he became the youngest person ever elected to the National Institute of Arts and Letters and toured Eastern Europe as part of a cultural exchange program with the Soviet Union as a guest of the State Department. In 1967, he and other American writers signed a letter urging Soviet writers to defend Jewish cultural institutions under attack by the Soviet government.

In 1968, Updike published *Couples*, a novel about adultery in a small fictional Massachusetts town called Tarbox. The book created a national sensation with its portrayal of the complicated relationships among a set of young married couples in the suburbs. It remained on the best-seller list for over a year and led to Updike's appearance on the cover of *Time* magazine underneath the headline: "The Adulterous Society."

Updike's fiction is distinguished by its attention to the concerns, passions and suffering of average Americans. His principal themes are religion, sex, America and death. "My subject is the American Protestant small-town middle class," Updike said in a 1966 interview. "I like middles. It is in the middles that extremes clash, where ambiguity restlessly rules." In the introduction to his book of short stories, *The Early Stories: 1953-1975*, he wrote that his goal was always "to give the mundane its beautiful due."

In 1974, he separated from Mary and moved to Boston, where he taught briefly at Boston University. In 1976, the Updikes were divorced and the following year he married Martha Ruggles Bernhard, settling with her and her three children first in Georgetown, Massachusetts, and then in Beverly Farms, Masschusetts.

Among the dozen or so novels he published in the next quarter century, one of the most popular was *The Witches of Eastwick* (1984), a playful novel about witches living in Rhode Island. It was celebrated by some as an exuberant sexual comedy and a satirical view of women's liberation. He described it as an attempt to "make things right with my, what shall we call them, 'feminist detractors'." It was made into a major motion picture in 1987, directed by George Miller and starring Jack Nicholson with Cher, Michelle Pfeiffer and Susan Sarandon as the three witches. The film won a number of awards and got mixed reviews. The majority of critics saw the film as a showcase for the comic talents of Nicholson.

Updike returned to the witches in another novel, *The Widows of Eastwick* (2008), portraying them as widows revisiting the town no longer preying on men as they once did but instead as ordinary women haunted by the sins of their youth.

Rabbit, Run was also made into a film in 1970 by Warner Brothers. The film starred James Caan and Carrie Snodgrass and had its world premiere in Updike's

Memorial to the great author from Reading who created the legendary character Harry "Rabbit" Angstrom.

hometown of Reading. Early reaction was negative and Warner Brothers aborted a wide release.

John Updike died of lung cancer at a hospice in Danvers, Massachusetts on January 27, 2009 at the age of 76. He published over 60 books in his lifetime and is considered one of the greatest American fiction writers of his generation. He won numerous awards for his work, and in 2008 he was selected by the National Endowment for the Humanities to present the Jefferson Lecture, the U.S. government's highest humanities-related honor.

Shortly after his death, the John Updike Society was founded. In 2010, it announced the establishment of the John Updike Society Archive at Alvernia University in Reading, and held its first Biennial Society Conference in Reading. In 2012, the Society purchased Updike's childhood home at 117 Philadelphia Avenue in Shillington, with plans to turn it into a museum. A much anticipated biography of John Updike by Adam Begley was published in 2014.

Updike was cremated and initially his ashes were placed in a cremation garden in Manchester, Massachusetts near his home. In 2011, his family decided to memorialize him in Pennsylvania as well. Some of his remains are buried in Robeson Lutheran Church Cemetery in Plowville.

If You Go:

The marker at John Updike's memorial is unusual and interesting. The marker was carved by his son, Michael. The names on the front of the marker are the various ways he was referred to in life: "Johnny" was what he was called by his parents and grandparents; "John" was how he was addressed by friends and lovers; "Dad" by his children; "Grandpa" by his grandsons; "John Updike," his professional moniker; and "J.H.U." the way he signed his early cartoons. On the back of the slate is a poem Updike wrote when he was 16 and was rejected by *The New Yorker*.

28.
The Smooth Jazzman

Grover Washington Jr.
County: Montgomery
Town: Bala Cynwyd
Cemetery: West Laurel Hill Cemetery
Address: 215 Belmont Avenue

He grew up surrounded by music. He would become one of the most popular soul and jazz saxophonist of all time. He would write much of his own material and later be recognized as an arranger and a producer. He is widely considered to be one of the founders of the smooth jazz genre. While some jazz critics found his music to be simplistic, he became one of the most commercially successful saxophonists in history. His name was Grover Washington Jr.

Washington was born in Buffalo, New York on December 12, 1943. His father played the saxophone and was a collector of jazz records. His mother was in the church choir. He grew up listening to his father's records. When he was ten years old his dad gave him a saxophone. He would practice on his own and by the time he was twelve he was playing in clubs.

As he grew older Washington played with a group from the Midwest who went by the clever name The Four Clefts. His next band was called the Mark III Trio. He was then drafted into the U. S. Army. It was in the army that he met a drummer from New York by the name of Billy Cobham. Cobham was an established New York musician and he introduced Washington to other musicians from the big apple. After he was discharged Washington exhibited his talents in New York before heading to Philadelphia in 1967 where he became closely identified with that city. Leon Spencer released two albums in the early 70's and Washington appeared on both.

Then Washington caught a break when another sax musician was unable to make a recording date. Washington stepped in and played impressively. This led to Washington's first solo album "Inner City Blues." The record showcased his talent with the soprano, alto, tenor and baritone saxophones. He was becoming known as an up and coming jazz artist.

In the early 70's he released three albums that made him a force in the world of jazz and soul music. In 1974 he released his fourth album "Mister Magic" and it became a major commercial success. The record made it to number 10 on the Billboard charts and the title track made it to number 16 on the R&B singles chart. His next album "Feels So Good" also made it to number 10 on Billboard.

In the late 70's Washington signed with Elektra Records which was part of the Warner Music Group. In 1980 he released "Winelight" the record that many believe to represent his best effort. Washington loved basketball and he was a big fan of the Philadelphia 76ers which led to him dedicating the second track on the record "Let It Flow" to Julius Erving. He also occasionally played the national anthem prior to the

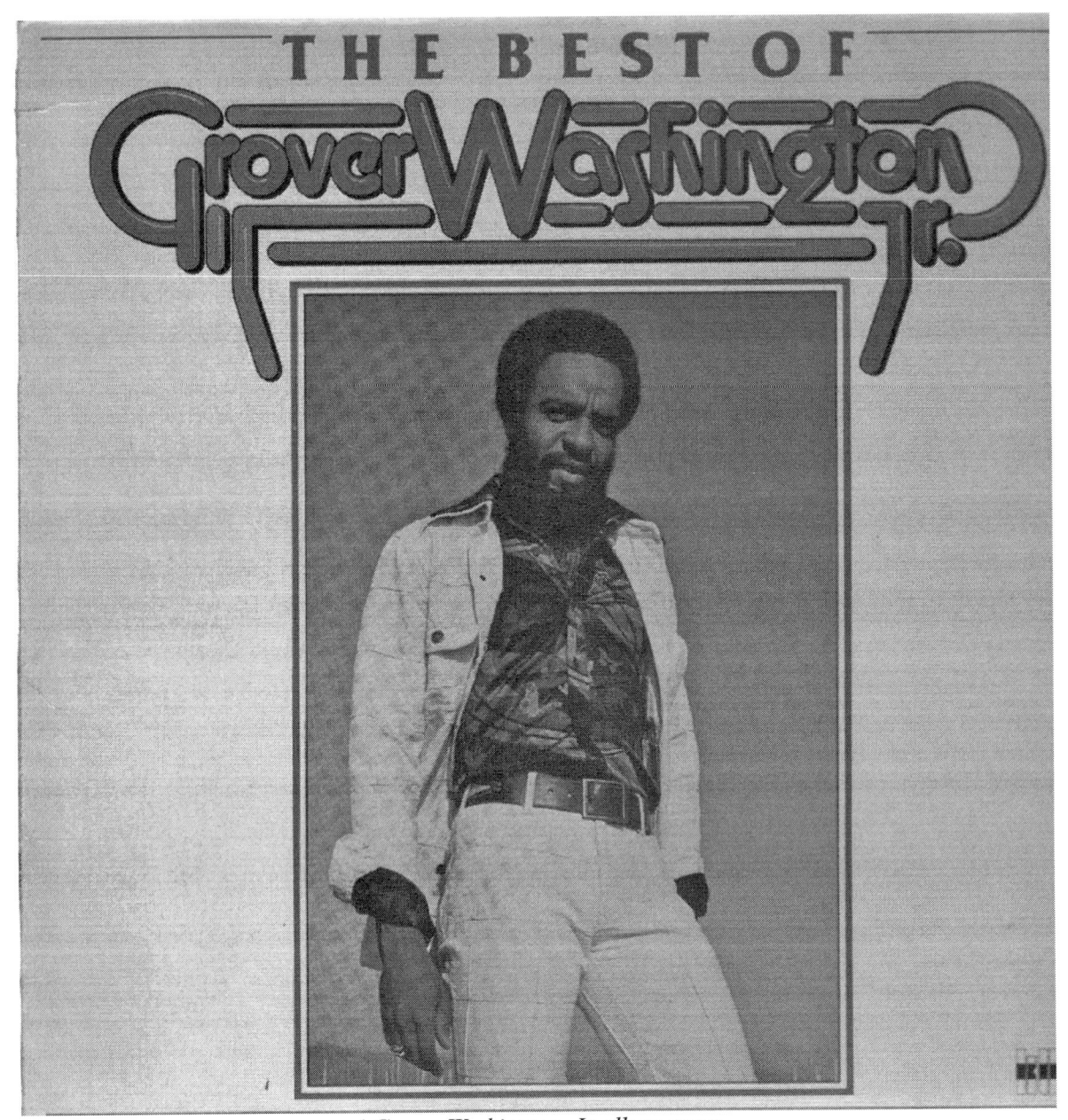

A Grover Washington, Jr. album cover

76ers games. The high point of the album "Winelight" was his work with the soul artist Bill Withers on the song "Just The Two of Us." That song was a major hit and reached number 2 on the charts and won a Grammy in 1982 for Best R&B Song, it was also a Song of the Year nominee. The album which went platinum won the Grammy for Best Jazz Fusion Performance. "Winelight" was also nominated for record of the year.

In the 1980's Washington moved toward the jazz mainstream. Among the artists he worked with was Herbie Hancock. He also released the first album of music from the "Cosby Show." During a 1989 interview Washington said, "There's a record player

Grave site of the noted smooth jazz man.

playing in here all the time." At the time he was pointing at his head. "I'm listening to everything. The screech of brakes. Three or four people walking and you can hear their heels clicking. Railroad tracks."

In 1996, he played at President Clinton's 50th birthday celebration at Radio City Music Hall. Clinton later said, "Grover Washington was as versatile as any jazz musician in America moving with ease and fluency from vintage jazz to funk, and from gospel to blues to pop." Washington once said, "I want to be able to visit any genre and converse there with my horn." Noting that quote Clinton added, "Grover Washington did exactly that, and beautifully."

On December 17, 1999, Washington performed four songs for the "Saturday Early Show" on CBS. While waiting in the green room he collapsed and was rushed to a local New York hospital where he died that evening. It was determined that he had suffered a massive heart attack. He was laid to rest in West Laurel Hill Cemetery. He was 56 years old.

If You Go:

See Chapter 19's "If You Go" section in this volume.

Anthony Wayne

29.
Mad Anthony

Anthony Wayne
County: (i) Erie and (ii) Delaware
Town: (i) Erie and (ii) Wayne
Cemetery: (i) Garrison Hill and (ii) Old St. David's Church Cemetery
Address: (i) Ash Street and (ii) 763 South Valley Forge Road

Anthony Wayne was a United States Army general in the American Revolutionary War and a statesman who is buried in two places. Had he not died suddenly at the age of 51, he might have given John Adams or Thomas Jefferson a real challenge for the Presidency in 1796 and 1800.

Wayne was born on New Years Day 1745 in Chester County, Pennsylvania, and attended a private school in Philadelphia operated by his uncle. He eventually became an excellent surveyor and in 1765 was sent to Nova Scotia as a financial agent and surveyor in the service of a real estate company on the recommendation of Benjamin Franklin. He returned to the United States in 1767, married, and continued in his profession as well as serving in several local offices. In 1774, his father Isaac died and Anthony inherited his father's prosperous tannery business. Also that year, he was chosen as one of the provincial representatives to consider the relations between the colonies and Great Britain, and was a member of the Pennsylvania convention that was held in Philadelphia to discuss this matter.

Wayne served in the Pennsylvania legislature in 1775. He was fond of military affairs. He began studying works on the art of war, and at the onset of the Revolutionary War raised a militia. In 1776, Wayne became colonel of the 4th Pennsylvania regiment. He and his regiment were part of the Continental Army's failed invasion of Canada. He attacked the British at the Battle of Three Rivers and although wounded and defeated, withdrew his troops creditably and then was ordered to assume command at Fort Ticonderoga.

In February 1777, Wayne was commissioned a brigadier general. Prior to the war, Wayne had no military experience and other more experienced officers resented his quick advancement. He became known for his bravado and ill-advised attacks. He earned the nickname "Mad" Anthony Wayne because of his impulsive actions on the battlefield. Wayne was known for his fiery temper and would rather attack the enemy than avoid them.

Later in 1777, he assisted George Washington in the failed defense of the nation's capitol, Philadelphia. He commanded troops at Brandywine, Germantown and Paoli. The British surprise attack at Paoli on September 20, 1777, was a dark moment for Wayne. He lost a lot of men, and some of his officers thought he handled it poorly. Wayne's temper took hold, and he demanded first an official inquiry and then a full court martial. The court martial unanimously exonerated Wayne and acquitted him "with the highest honor." Washington heartily approved.

General Anthony Wayne, after portrait by Charles Willson Peale. The General's portrait was painted c. 1783 with him in full Revolutionary War uniform,

Washington relied heavily on Wayne throughout the war. Before making strategic decisions, it was Washington's habit to have his top generals write out their suggestions. He could always count on Wayne to propose aggressive and well thought-out plans.

During the winter of 1777-78, Wayne did much to supply the American camp at Valley Forge. In March, he made a successful raid into British lines, capturing horses, cattle and other needed supplies. In June of 1778, he led the American attack at the Battle of Monmouth. It was the first time Americans held their own in toe-to-toe battle with the British troops.

The highlight of Wayne's Revolutionary War service was his victory at Stony Point, New York on July 16, 1779. Washington had asked Wayne to form and command an elite "American Light Corps" (the equivalent of today's Special Forces). Wayne led his troops in a carefully planned, nighttime, surprise attack against a heavily fortified stronghold on top of a steep Hudson River palisade. The assault was successful and Wayne's troops captured the fort and its occupants. Before dawn, Wayne sent Washington a message that read: "The fort and garrison with Colonel Johnston are ours. Our officers and men behaved like men who are determined to be free."

The assault at Stony Point was widely recognized as one of the most brilliant maneuvers of the war. Congress unanimously passed resolutions praising Wayne and awarded him a gold medal commemorative. The Continental Army had experienced few successes. This victory, led personally by General Wayne, substantially improved the soldiers' morale.

In 1780, Wayne helped put down a mutiny of 1,300 Pennsylvania men who had not received payment from the government. He did so by serving as the men's advocate before the Confederation Congress, where he arranged an agreement to the advantage of the government and the satisfaction of the men.

In the summer of 1781 just before the Battle of Yorktown, Wayne saved a Continental Army force led by the Marquis de Lafayette from a trap set by the commander of the British Army, Lieutenant General Lord Cornwallis, near Williamsburg, Virginia. Wayne's small contingent of 800 Pennsylvanians was the vanguard of the continental forces. They were crossing over a swamp by a narrow causeway when they were ambushed by over 4,000 British. Instead of retreating, Wayne charged. The unexpected maneuver so surprised the enemy that they fell back confused allowing the rest of Lafayette's command to avoid the trap.

After the British surrender at Yorktown on October 19, 1781, Wayne went further south and severed the British alliance with Native American tribes in Georgia. He negotiated peace treaties with both the Creek and Cherokee, for which Georgia rewarded him with the gift of a large rice plantation. In October 1783 he was promoted to major general and retired from the Continental Army.

Wayne returned to Pennsylvania and resumed his civilian life. In 1784, he was elected to the general assembly from Chester County and served in the convention that ratified the Constitution of the United States. He then moved to Georgia and was elected to the Second United States Congress in 1791. He lost that seat during a debate over his residency qualifications and declined to run for reelection.

President Washington showed his high regard for Wayne once again in 1792 when he recalled him from civilian life and appointed Wayne as the commanding general of the newly-formed "Legion of the United States." At the end of the Revolutionary War, Great Britain agreed that the Mississippi River would be the Western boundary of the United States and that the Great Lakes would be the northern border. Presumably this meant British troops would withdraw from these areas into Canada. In fact, they did not. They encouraged and supplied a Western Indian Confederacy led by Blue Jacket of the Shawnees and Little Turtle of the Miamis. The Indians had achieved major victories over U.S. forces in 1790 under command of General Josiah Harmar and in 1791 under command of General Arthur St. Clair. More than 700 Americans died in the fighting.

Wayne recruited troops from the Pittsburgh area and established a basic training facility at Legionville to prepare the men of the "Legion of the United States" for battle. Located in Beaver County, Legionville was the first facility ever established to provide basic training for U.S. Army recruits.

In August 1794, Wayne mounted an assault on the Indian confederacy at the Battle of Fallen Timbers near Toledo, Ohio. It was a decisive victory for the U.S. forces and ended for all time the power of the British on American soil.

Wayne then negotiated the Treaty of Greenville between the Indian tribes and the United States. The treaty was signed in August 1795 and gave most of what is now Ohio to the United States. He returned home to a hero's welcome in the Philadelphia area.

In June 1796, Wayne was back in the frontier overseeing the surrender of British forts to the U.S. In a visit to Fort Presque Isle in Erie, Pennsylvania, he suffered a serious gout attack. There were no physicians at the fort and calls went out to Pittsburgh and the Army hospitals. Unfortunately, help arrived too late, and Anthony Wayne died on December 15, 1796.

A year earlier at Fort Presque Isle, to assist in defending against attacks from Native Americans, 200 Federal troops from Wayne's army under the direction of Captain John Grubb built a blockhouse on a bluff there known as Garrison Hill. Wayne had requested that upon his death he be buried there. When he died, his body was placed in a plain oak coffin, his initials and date of death were driven into the wood using round-headed brass tacks, and his request was honored: he was buried at the foot of the blockhouse's flagstaff on Garrison Hill.

Twelve years later, Wayne's son, Isaac, rode to Erie in a small, two-wheeled carriage called a "sulky." He came (at the urging of his sister Peggy) to bring his father's remains back to be buried in the family plot at St. David's Church about 400 miles away outside of Philadelphia. Young Wayne enlisted the help of Dr. J.G. Wallace, who had been with Mad Anthony at the Battle of Fallen Timbers and at his side when he died.

The blockhouse where Wayne died and he was originally buried.

When Wallace opened Wayne's coffin, he found little decay except in the lower portion of one leg. This caused a dilemma, as Isaac did not have enough space to transport the entire body. He expected to put bones in boxes on his sulky. Dr. Wallace used a custom common to American Indians to solve the dilemma. He dismembered the body and boiled it in a large iron kettle until the flesh dropped off. He cleaned the bones and packed them into Isaac's boxes. The task was so distasteful that Dr. Wallace threw the remaining tissue and his instruments into the coffin and closed the grave. Isaac Wayne made the long journey across Pennsylvania with his father's bones in the back of his sulky. The bones were interred at Old St. David's Church Cemetery with funeral rites celebrated on July 4, 1809. A huge crowd attended.

General Anthony Wayne is well-memorialized. He has a long list of cities, towns and municipalities named after him, including 15 states that have a Wayne County. In Pennsylvania, there is a Wayne County as well as a Waynesboro and a Waynesburg. He has schools, bridges, a university (Wayne State University in Detroit), a brewing company (Mad Anthony Brewing Co. in Fort Wayne, Indiana), an ale (Mad Anthony Ale, a product of Erie Brewing Co.), a hotel (General Wayne Inn in Merion, PA), parks, hospitals and even a barber shop named in his honor. There is a large statue in Fort Wayne, Indiana, as well as a gilded bronze equestrian statue at the Philadelphia Museum of Art and one at Valley Forge. In 1929, the U.S. Post Office issued a stamp honoring Wayne and commemorating the 150th anniversary of the Battle of Fallen Timbers.

If You Go:

Anthony Wayne's strange interment has given rise to a popular **ghost story**. It was a long, tough trip from Erie to Wayne over 380 miles of unpaved roads of what is now Route 322. The story goes that Isaac had many problems along the way and that the trunk kept falling off and breaking open, losing bones along the way. Some claim that on each New Year's Day (Wayne's birthday), his ghost rises from his grave in Wayne and rides across the state searching for his missing bones. The kettle used to boil Wayne's body and the dissection instruments used by Dr. Wallace are on display at the Erie County History Center on State Street in Erie.

The original grave site of "Mad" Anthony Wayne.

Very nearby is **Erie Cemetery**, which contains the graves of a number of interesting people, including famous Civil War General **Strong Vincent**, who was a hero at the Battle of Gettysburg where he died; **Harry Burleigh**, the internationally known African-American baritone and composer who composed such spirituals as "Swing Low Sweet Chariot" and "Nobody Knows the Trouble I've Seen;" **Andrew Forbeck**, a Congressional Medal of Honor recipient from the Philippine Insurrection; and **Samuel Jethroe**, who was the oldest man to win baseball's Rookie of the Year award in 1950 at the age of 32.

About 15 miles outside of Erie is the small town of **Girard**, which is home to the **Battles Bank Gallery**. Battles was a bank until the late 1980's but its owner, **Charlotte Elizabeth Battles**, brought much attention to Girard when she defied President Roosevelt's order to close in 1933. She sent a note to FDR saying "Mr. President, we're minding our business, you do the same. Since I do not presume to tell you how to run the country, please do not presume to tell me how to run my bank." Ms. Battles, who died in 1952, is buried in **Girard Cemetery**.

The **Girard Borough Building** contains a statue of a dog that is an interesting grave story. For over 100 years the statue of a dog named "**Shep**" had stood vigilantly over the grave of his master, **H.C. Davis**, who died in 1881. Shep died of poisoning in 1884 and was buried in the same plot. Mrs. Davis commissioned the statue in 1889 using a photograph to sculpt a life-sized figure of Shep sitting in a captain's chair. The statue was placed to mark the family plot in 1890. On September 30, 1993, the statue of Shep suddenly disappeared, the victim of an apparent theft. The town was stunned and angered. A reward fund was organized and flyers bearing a picture of the statue

This is the caldron of death where Wayne's son boiled the body down to the bare bones.

were distributed nationwide. Despite these efforts, local police went years without a lead in the case.

In 1997, Girard police received a phone call from an antique dealer in New Haven, Connecticut. The dealer had recently purchased a statue matching the description on the flyer. The police investigated and found the statue had traveled through antique dealers in Pennsylvania, Ohio, New York, Maine and Connecticut. The police never solved the case as the first buyer of the statue had passed away in 1995. The dealer graciously agreed to return the statue to Girard and many in town were delighted. Once back in his hometown, Shep was donated by the descendants of the dog's owner to the Borough of Girard. Today, Shep remains on display in the lobby of the Girard Borough Municipal Building.

There are also interesting people buried at **Old St. David's Church Cemetery** (sometimes referred to today as St. David's Episcopal Church or simply "Old Saint David's") in the town of **Wayne**. Two of note are **William Wallace Atterbury** and **Richard Norris Williams**.

Known as the "Railroad General" in World War I, Atterbury was operating vice-president of the Pennsylvania Railroad at the outbreak of the war and reorganized the European railroad network to create rapid movement of allied troops and equipment that contributed greatly to victory. He was awarded medals by the United States, France, England, Serbia and Romania. He appeared on the cover of Time Magazine in February 1933.

R. Norris Williams (as he was generally known) was a champion tennis player, a Titanic survivor, and the great-great-grandson of Benjamin Franklin. He won two U.S. Open singles championships in 1914 and 1916. He also was on the victorious American Davis Cup teams in 1925 and 1926, and at the 1924 Olympics in Paris he won a gold medal in mixed doubles. All of this came after surviving the Titanic disaster, where his father with whom he was traveling died. His story is amazing and the subject of another chapter in this book. Williams was inducted into the International Tennis Hall of Fame in 1957.

Memorial marks one of the grave sites that hold the remains of a hero of the American Revolution Mad Anthony Wayne.

UNUSUAL TOMBSTONES

Civil War veteran George Mears

Honoring 57 Irish raolroad workers who died while building the Philadelphia and Columbia Railroad

Tragic ... so beautiful and so young ...

Another young lady and a beautiful poem ...

Someone who loved his Potter County cabin ...

One big cross ...

The "reliquary" of Jean Auguste Gisard

Here lies two great women ...

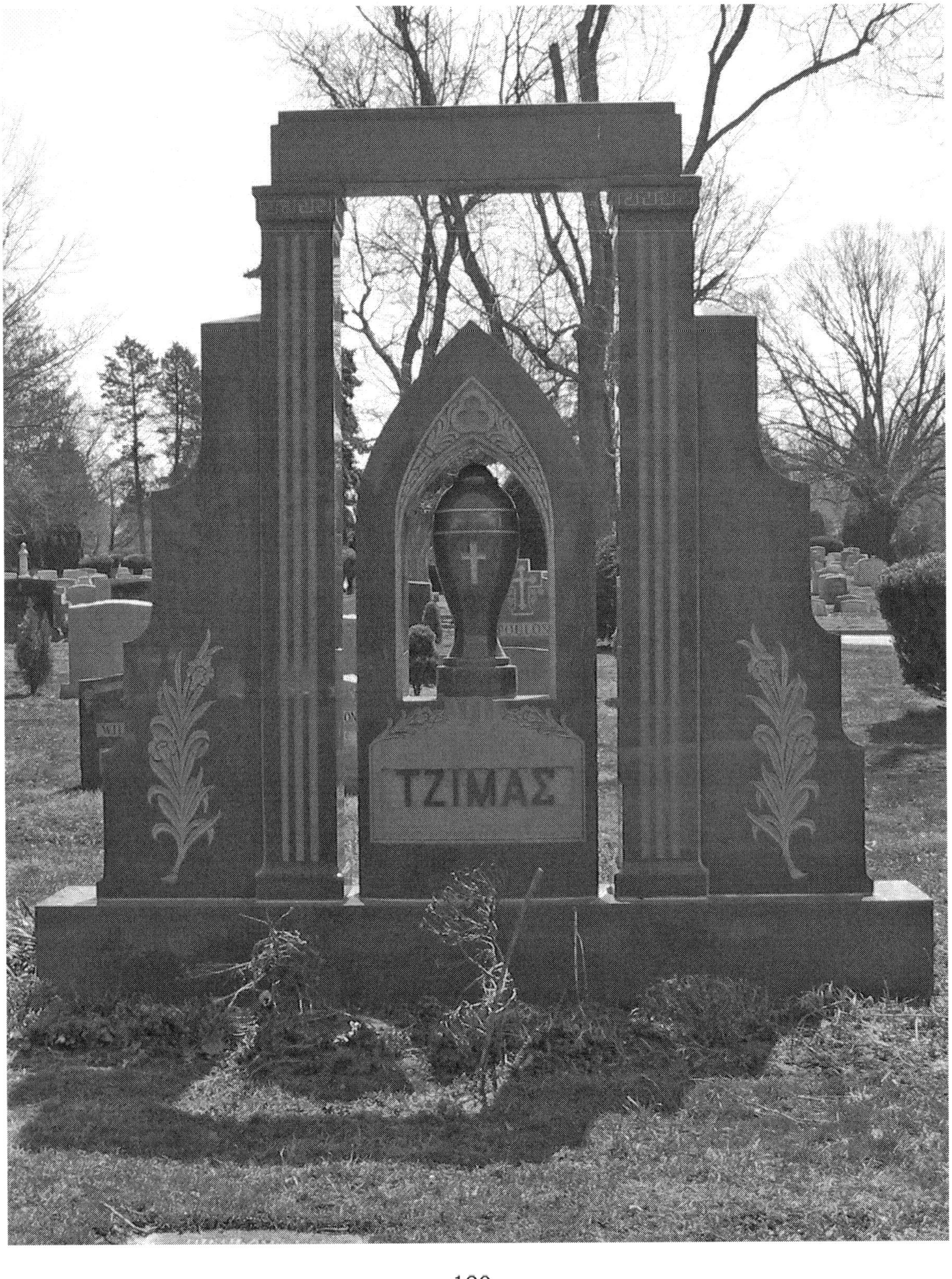
ΤΖΙΜΑΣ

A real trumpet?

INDEX

Adams, John, 165
Adams, Nick, 3 - 6
Anderson, Marion, 7 – 10
Angleton, James, 90
Ali, Muhammad, 51, 53 – 56
Atzerodt, George, 68
Bach, Joe, 114
Baer, John, 23,128
Barrymore, Drew, 19, 20
Barrymore, John, 17 – 20
Barrymore, Lionel, 17, 19, 20, 120
Begala, Paul, 21
Bell, Alexander Graham, 119
Bell, Bert, 115
Beyer, Hillary, 70
Blanda, George, 145, 147
Bork, Robert, 125, 126
Bradlee, Ben, 87, 90
Brady, Jim, 119
Bruno, Joseph, 75, 77, 78
Bruno, Philip, 75, 77, 78
Buchanan, James, 74
Burleigh, 169
Bush, George, 126
Butkus, Dick, 115
Cameron, Simon, 69
Caan, James, 159
Cappelletti, John, 94
Carville, James, 21, 23
Cash, Johnny, 5
Casey, Bob, 21 – 25, 126
Cher, 159
Clinton, Bill, 126, 163
Cobb, Ty, 151, 152
Conn, Billy, 113
Connally, John, 124, 125
Conrad, Robert, 6
Costner, Kevin, 125
Cox, Billy, 45, 47, 48
Crosby, Bing, 27, 28
Crowley, James, 25
Curtin, Andrew, 100
Daugherty, Duffy, 145
Day, Doris, 20
Dean, James, 5, 6
Dempsey, Jack, 63, 64

Dorsey, Jimmy, 26 – 29
Dorsey Tommy, 27 – 29
Earle, George, 77
Einstein, Albert, 9
Eisenhower, Dwight, 9
Engle, Rip, 94
Erving, Julius, 161
Ewbank, Weeb, 94
Fields, W. C., 20
Flaherty, Pete, 21
Flood, Dan, 25
Flynn, Errol, 20
Fonda, Henry, 3
Forbeck, Andrew, 169
Foreman, George, 55
Foster, Stephen, 121
Fox, Nellie, 45 – 47, 49
Franklin, Benjamin, 165
Frazier, Joe, 51 – 56
Garrison, Jim, 125
Garroway, Dave, 57 – 60
Gavin, Pud, 65
Geary, John, 69
Gibson, Josh, 121
Goodell, Roger, 128
Gorshin, Frank, 65
Greb, Harry, 61-65
Hagen, Walter, 81, 83
Hafer, Barbara, 24
Halas, George, 147
Hancock, Herbie, 162
Hancock, Winfield Scott, 70
Harding, Warren, 120
Hartranft, John, 66-70
Hayes, Rutherford, 69, 70
Heinz, John, 24, 125
Herold, David, 68
Hershey, Milton, 143
Hess, Anna Mary 71, 73
Hess, Robert, 71-74
Hewes, Joseph, 36, 37, 39, 43
Hill, Anita, 126
Hopkinson, Francis, 37 -39, 44
Hornsby, Rogers, 154
Houston, Whitney, 104
Irvin, Michael, 95
Janney, Peter, 88, 90
Jethroe, Samuel, 169

Johnson, Andrew, 67
Johnson, Jimmy, 95
Johnson Lyndon, 125
Johnson, Walter, 151, 154
Kehoe, Jack, 69, 78
Kelly, Jim, 145
Kennedy, Jackie, 87
Kennedy, John F., 85, 87-89, 91, 123-125
Kennedy, Robert, 21, 89
Kennedy, Ted, 125
Kopechne, Mary Jo, 25
LaBelle, Patti, 101
Lawrence, David, 65, 77
Leary, Timothy, 88
Lee, Robert E., 67
Lombardi, Vince, 93
Louis, Joe, 113
Mack, Connie, 45-47, 56, 84
Marino, Dan, 145
Mathewson, Christy, 151
Mathis, Buster, 51, 53
Mayer, Louis, 20
McDowell, Irvin, 67
McDermott, John, 79-83
McQueen, Steve, 5
Melvin, Harold, 101, 102
Meyer, Cord, 85, 87, 91
Meyer, Mary Pinchot, 85-91
Mifflin, Thomas, 74
Miller, Glenn, 27
Mineo, Sal, 6
Montana, Joe, 145
Moon, Warren, 147
Muldoon, William, 64
Murphy, Eddie, 103
Namath, Joe, 145
Nicholson, 159
Nixon, Richard, 94
Noakes, Cordelia, 11, 12, 14
Noakes, Dewilla, 11, 12, 14
Noakes, Elmo, 11, 12, 14
Osbourne, Tom, 96
Oswald, Lee Harvey, 123, 124
Paine, Lewis, 68
Page, Joe, 148
Palance, Jack, 3
Palmer, Arnold, 83
Pastor, Tony, 117

Paterno, Joe, 92-99
Paterno, Sue, 95
Pendergrass, Teddy, 101-104
Pfeiffer, Michelle, 159
Pierce, Winifred, 11 – 16
Pinchot, Gifford, 85, 88, 91
Pitcher, Molly, 16, 106-111
Presley, Elvis, 5, 28
Quimet, Francis, 81, 83
Ray, Ted, 81
Reagan, Ronald, 125
Reese, Pee Wee, 49
Rice, Grantland, 63, 81
Robinson, Jackie, 49, 147
Rockne, Knute, 113
Rooney, Art, 112-116
Roosevelt, Eleanor, 9
Ross, George, 37, 40, 43
Rush, Benjamin, 37, 41 – 43
Russell, Lillian, 117-121
Ruth, Babe, 151
Sandusky, Jerry, 96, 98
Sarandon, Susan, 159
Scranton, Bill, 21, 23
Sedgwick, Norma, 11, 14
Selznick, David, 20
Shapp, Milton, 21
Shugart, Randall, 16
Snodgrass, Carrie, 159
Specter, Arlen, 122-128
Stengel, Casey, 49
Stevens, Thaddeus, 74
Stone, Oliver, 125
Stuhldreher, Harry, 65
Surrant, Mary, 68
Sutherland, Jack, 155
Testaverde, Vinnie, 95
Thaw, Harry, 121
Titanic Victims and Survivors, 129-144
Thomas, Clarence, 125, 126
Thornburgh, Dick, 24, 125
Thorpe, Jim, 78
Thrower, Willie, 145-148
Toomey, Pat, 126, 127
Traynor, Pie, 115, 151-155
Tunney, Gene, 61, 63-65
Turrentine, Stanley, 121
Unitas, Johnny, 115, 145
Updike, John, 156-160

Van Zeist, Louis, 84
Vardon, Harry, 81
Vincent, Strong, 169
Wagner, Honus, 149-152
Walters, Barbara, 59
Washington, George, 39, 41, 108, 111, 165-167
Washington, Grover, 104, 161-163
Washington, Martha, 107
Wayne, Anthony, 165-171
White, Byron "Whizzer", 114
Wofford, Harris, 24, 25
Wood, Natalie, 5 - 6

Cemeteries

Allegheny Cemetery, 117, 120, 121
Arlington Cemetery, 135, 136, 144
Annunciation of the Blessed Virgin Cemetery, 27, 29
Calvary Cemetery, 61, 65
Christ Church Burial Ground, 37, 39, 41, 44
Christ Our Redeemer Cemetery, 113, 116
Church of the Redeemer Cemetery, 140, 143
Eden Cemetery, 7
Erie Cemetery, 169
Flight 93 Crash Site, 30, 32, 35
Garrison Hill, 165, 167, 168
Greenwood Memorial Park, 145, 148
Holy Cross Cemetery, 79, 84
Holy Sepulcher Cemetery, 56
Ivy Hill Cemetery, 51, 56
Jefferson Memorial Park, 149, 152, 155
Laurel Hill Cemetery, 134, 135, 138
Milford Cemetery, 85, 91
Montgomery Cemetery, 67
Mount Vernon Cemetery, 17
Newport Cemetery, 45, 50
Old Public Graveyard, 16, 107, 111

Old Saint David's Churchyard, 136, 138, 143, 165, 168, 170
Robeson Lutheran Church Cemetery, 157, 160
Shalom memorial Park, 123
Spring Creek Presbyterian Cemetery, 93, 98
St. Catherine's Cemetery, 21, 25
Sts. Cyril and Methodius Ukrainian Cemetery, 3, 6
St. Michael's Cemetery, 139
St. Patrick's Cemetery, 75
Sts. Peter and Paul Cemetery, 132, 144
Saint Stanislaus's Polish Catholic Cemetery, 78
St. Thomas Town Cemetery, 45, 47
Sunset View Cemetery, 132
West Green Tree Church of the Brethren, 71, 74
West Laurel Hill Cemetery, 57, 60, 101, 104, 139, 142, 143, 161, 163
Westminster Memorial Gardens, 11, 14, 16
Westmorland County Memorial Park, 133
Union Cemetery, 100
Union Cemetery of Whitemarsh, 131
Valley Forge Memorial Gardens, 139

Cities and Towns

Altoona, 12, 15, 69
Ardmore, 83
Atascadero, 111
Atlantic City, 64
Bala Cynwyd, 57, 60, 101, 104, 139, 142, 161
Baltimore, 47
Beaufort, 51
Bellefonte, 100
Berwick, 3, 6
Benton Harbor, 63
Birdsboro, 139, 140

Boston, 119, 159
Brookline, 81
Brooklyn, 93
Bryn Mawr, 140
Buffalo, 81, 161
Byberry, 41
Cambridge, 87
Carlisle, 11, 13, 44, 107-109
Chambersburg, 45, 47
Chicago, 17, 57, 59, 79, 117
Cleveland, 50, 64
Clinton, 117
Collingdale, 7
Coulter, 113
Danbury, 9
Drexel Hill, 135
Duncansville, 12
Elizabethtown, 71, 74
Elkins Park, 139
Englewood, 93
Erie, 165, 169
Flourtown, 131
Frederick, 45
Freehold, 108
Garkida, 72
Georgetown, 86, 87, 89
Germantown, 142
Greensburg, 133
Harrisburg, 50
Hazleton, 78
Hometowns of the Flight 93 Crew and Passengers, 34, 35
Honolulu, 57
Huntingdon Valley, 123
Jersey City, 3
Jim Thorpe, 78
Kelayres, 75, 77
King of Prussia, 139
Lancaster, 74
Latrobe, 94, 148
Lisbon, 109
London, 9, 117, 131, 157
Los Angeles, 3, 4
Lower Burrell, 145, 148
Manchester, 160
Manila, 55
Mauch Chunk, 69
McAdoo, 75, 77
McVeytown, 12, 15

Milford, 85, 88, 91
Moscow, 21
Mount Joy, 71, 74
Nanticoke, 3
Newark, 31
New Cumberland, 11
New Kensington, 145
Newport, 45, 47, 50
Newville, 16
New York City, 3, 9, 21, 30, 31, 33, 51, 57, 63, 64, 77, 85, 93, 105, 115, 117, 129, 135, 137, 140, 147, 148, 163
Nitrp, 152
Norristown, 67
Paris, 59, 137
Penn Hills, 132
Petersburg, 67
Philadelphia, 7, 10, 13, 17, 20, 37, 39, 41, 44, 51, 56, 69, 79, 84, 101, 103, 104, 107, 114, 123, 126, 128, 133-135, 137, 138, 165
Plowville, 157, 160
Pittsburgh, 57, 61, 65, 68, 113, 115-117, 120, 132, 149, 152, 154, 167
Pottsville, 69, 77
Princeton, 37
Reading, 69, 157, 160
Red Bank, 111
Richmond, 67
Ridley Park, 133
Rome, 59
Roseville, 12
Russell, 123
Saint Louis, 57
Saint Thomas, 45, 47
Salt Lake City, 12
San Francisco, 17, 31, 85
Scranton, 21
Schenectady, 57, 67
Shanksville, 31, 32
Shawnee-on-the-Delaware, 81
Shenandoah, 27, 29
Shippensburg, 111
Somerset, 30

Somerville, 152
Southampton, 129
Springfield, 132,133
Springville, 12
State College, 93, 98
Steubenville,132
Swarthmore, 59
Tarentum, 147
Tokyo, 53, 90
Toledo, 167
Valley Forge, 107, 166
Waka, 72
Wandali, 72
Washington, 31, 67, 87, 88, 90, 119
Wayne, 136, 138, 165, 169
Wichita, 123
Williamsburg, 167
Wilmington, 37
Yeadon, 79, 83

Pubs and Restaurants

Battered Mug, 78
Gus's Keystone Family Restaurant, 74
Miller's Ale House, 128
Molly Maguire Pub, 78
Newport Hotel and Tavern, 50
O'Donnell Winery, 6
Piccolo Forno, 121
Rustic Tavern, 16
Woodlands Inn and Conference Center, 25

Made in the USA
Lexington, KY
14 July 2014